PRAISE FOR
FULLY ALIVE

"This book is a wake-up call for those sleepwalking through life. In this powerful book, Ken Davis shares his personal struggles with candor and humor. He then points the way to a life that is fuller and richer than most of us could imagine. If you think your life is almost over, think again. Ken will convince you it is just beginning."

—MICHAEL HYATT
CHAIRMAN, THOMAS NELSON PUBLISHERS
AUTHOR, *PLATFORM: GET NOTICED IN A NOISY WORLD*

"I am profoundly grateful for the impact that Ken has had and continues to have on my life. He is a brilliant speaker, a profound communicator, and a dear friend. If you are ready to start living fully alive, I highly recommend this book to you."

—SHEILA WALSH
AUTHOR, *GOD LOVES BROKEN PEOPLE: AND THOSE WHO PRETEND THEY'RE NOT.*

"'Between the cross and heaven, there's a whole lot of living going on.' I am convinced more than ever that each human life is meant to be lived out completely—fully alive. That is exactly what this book is all about. And I can think of no one on this planet who has tackled this theme more powerfully or with more heart than Ken Davis. *Fully Alive* is a must-read for anyone and most especially those tempted to believe that their best days have already been lived."

—BILL GAITHER

FULLY ALIVE

A Journey that Will Change Your Life

KEN DAVIS

W PUBLISHING GROUP

AN IMPRINT OF THOMAS NELSON

Published in Nashville, Tennessee, by W Publishing Group. W Publishing is a registered trademark of Thomas Nelson.

Thomas Nelson titles may be purchased in bulk for educational, business, fundraising, or sales promotional use. For information, please email SpecialMarkets@ThomasNelson.com.

ISBN: 978-0-7852-1811-1 (TP)
ISBN: 978-0-7852-3827-0 (IE)

Library of Congress Cataloging-in-Publication Data

Davis, Ken, 1946-
 Fully alive : a journey that will change your life / Ken Davis.
   p. cm.
 ISBN 978-0-8499-4842-8
 1. Christian life. 2. Life—Religious aspects—Christianity. I. Title.
 BV4509.5.D27 2012
 248.4—dc23

2012008645

This book is dedicated to the memory of Happy Pierce, who lived more fully alive in seventeen years than many people live in an entire lifetime.

CONTENTS

CONTENTS

ACKNOWLEDGMENTS

THANK YOU TO MY WIFE, DIANE, WHO OFTEN KNOCKED ON the door of my study as I wrote this book—to see if I was actually still alive. I love you.

Thank you to Kialee, Lexi, Jadyn, Tyler, Bailey, and Preston, six of the greatest grandchildren any man could hope for. You have been so patient as my attention has been focused on finishing this book. You have given me a glimpse of God's love.

Thank you to the Chaffee County Search and Rescue Squad and to Molly for helping us find the princess.

Thank you to John Perry for the hours editing and rewriting the manuscript and helping me bring it to life.

Thank you to Robert, Eric, and Andrew Wolgemuth for believing in me and in the message of *Fully Alive*.

Thank you to Joy Groblebe for her edits and hard work getting the details out of the way so I could concentrate on writing.

Thank you to Matt Baugher and the team at Thomas Nelson for their faithful support when the going got tough.

Thank you to my Lord for giving me a reason to live fully alive.

Chapter One

LOST

IT WAS THE END TO A PERFECT DAY. MY WIFE, DIANE, AND
I had driven with our three granddaughters up an old mining
road high into the mountains of Colorado and set up camp in a
little meadow at 10,500 feet. All day we rode ATV four-wheelers
on narrow trails that snaked above the tree line to abandoned
gold mines. We climbed to the tops of rocky ridges where we
could see for miles in every direction. I relished my role as hero,
trailblazer, and camping expert to the three little girls who
shared this adventure: Kialee, the studious competitive athlete; Lexi, the drama queen; and four-year-old Jadyn, part-time
affectionate princess and full-time nemesis to her sisters. The
girls in turn were experts at making me stop to see joy in the
little miracles of life.

My goal was to lead them to the top of the mountain. Their
goal was to enjoy the journey. They squealed with delight at every
clump of high country flowers and whooped with excitement
when I pointed out the chubby marmot watching from his rocky
sentinel. They collapsed in giggles when little pikas with big ears

squeaked in alarm and scurried off to dive for cover in the rocky crevices. Jadyn stayed close by my side, holding my hand, soaking in the wonder of it all. Even at age four she climbed fearlessly up steep slopes and rode narrow trails, eager to find whatever surprise waited around the next corner or over the next ridge.

After a long and exciting day, we returned to our cozy campsite to fix dinner. Every meal you can think of is a hundred times tastier when cooked over a campfire. That night we had filet mignon, known to noncampers as hot dogs. Dessert was s'mores. What a delight to watch the girls roast marshmallows! To a child a marshmallow on the end of a stick is an exotic torch. A beautifully browned marshmallow is boring, but smiles and shouts of joy erupt when the little white treats burst into flaming torches that can be waved dangerously around nearby siblings. The girls quickly mashed the charred blobs of marshmallow and a square of Hershey's chocolate between two graham crackers and swallowed them whole so they could light another torch.

When the marshmallows were gone, they poked their sticks into the coals until they began to burn. The glowing ember on the end of a stick became a magic pen for writing names and drawing elaborate designs in the inky sky. Finally eyelids began to droop. We allowed the fire to settle and then lay on our backs in the meadow, whispering of the beauty of the star-jeweled heavens. When you're at 10,500 feet on a clear night, the brightness of the stars hurts your eyes. A meteor streaked across the sky, sparking a minicelebration and marking time to call it a night. Diane and I tucked our treasures into toasty down sleeping bags and gave thanks for a magnificent day spent enjoying God's creation.

At the first hint of dawn, we awoke to the three amigas shaking us and shouting, "Wake up! Wake up and light another fire!" We were out of wood, so I slipped into cold, stiff clothing and icy boots to lead the girls on our first adventure of the day, gathering firewood. We looked for old, dead aspen trees, which are excellent for campfires. Many of these trees remain standing when they die. I knew we could easily push over the smaller ones and drag them back to camp.

I was concerned about our little princess, Jadyn. She could easily be hurt by even a small tree falling in the wrong direction. So as we crossed the old mining road, I handed her a fallen branch and said, "You can take this tree to your grandmother and help her start the fire." With obvious delight and pride she began dragging her personal "tree" back to camp. I can still see her struggling to get it across the road. When she was almost to the campsite, the other girls and I turned into the forest to search for bigger timber.

That was the last place I saw Jadyn.

TERROR

Evidently the princess got almost to her grandmother and then decided, *I would rather be with Grandpa.* Unknown to any of us, she dropped her tree, turned around to search for me—and wandered into the wilderness at 10,500 feet. When we returned with our supply of wood and began to prepare for breakfast, Diane asked, "Where's Jadyn?"

"Isn't she with you?" I replied.

Her eyes widened. "No! I thought she was with you!"

Panic! We exploded from the campsite in every direction, screaming Jadyn's name. In the first hour after she disappeared, I begged God for mercy as our search expanded. Obviously she had wandered far enough not to hear our calls. I ran as fast and as far as I could along every path I thought she might have taken. I retraced the steps we took to gather wood. Diane hopped on one of the ATVs and drove a mile up the mining road from our campsite and then a mile below. She paused often to stop the machine and call Jadyn's name. In the first stage of this kind of crisis, hope lingers in the midst of adrenaline-fueled panic. *Maybe with the next few steps I'll spot her pink matching outfit or a flash of that blonde hair. Maybe on the next breath of wind we'll hear her voice. Maybe she'll be where this road runs out. Oh, I hope she's not down by the river!*

After about two and a half hours I began to steel myself for the worst.

A green truck made its way up the road. It was a forest ranger who, when he heard the news, immediately called the Chaffee County rescue team. These amazing volunteers seemed to arrive almost instantly and began to organize a search. A child lost in this kind of wilderness is in a life-threatening situation. The sooner the search begins, the better the chances of finding the child. They had to find her—storm clouds were rolling in over the peaks. The temperature could drop to dangerous levels in minutes, and if it started to rain . . . I couldn't allow my mind to go there. Jadyn was my little partner, my little princess. I was her hero. She trusted me. I couldn't let her down.

As I stumbled through the undergrowth calling her name, I could see her trusting blue eyes looking out at me from every patch of brush. I remembered the prayer she had said on my behalf when I was very sick: "Please God, don't let my grandpa be afraid." Now my little prayer warrior was gone.

"Children don't go uphill." The rescue leader's briefing broke my train of thought. "When children are lost they take the easiest route downhill. Where did you last see Jadyn?"

I pointed to the spot, a small bush where she had crossed the road, dragging her personal tree. He took out a roll of pink survey ribbon, tore off a piece, and tied it to the bush. Pink ribbon!

Couldn't they have chosen any color but that one? Tears flowed freely down my face as the leader explained that his team would go about a mile above our camp and begin searching downhill from there. As they began to assemble for the search, another team member asked for some of Jadyn's personal items, bits of clothing that might give search dogs a scent they could follow. Diane and I were inconsolable.

There was no cell phone coverage in that remote area, so Diane headed down toward civilization to call Jadyn's parents and to ask our friends around the world to pray. Still sobbing, I went to search the creek that flowed behind our camp, bracing myself for what I might find. Half stumbling, half running, I shouted myself hoarse calling Jadyn's name as I followed the bank. After about a mile I saw the mining road. Surely if she had come this direction she would have seen the road and taken it rather than continuing on through the tangled brush that bordered the creek. It was then I remembered the swampy area farther up the mountain between the creek and the road—a stretch of bog covered with almost impenetrable brush and potholes full of mossy, stagnant water.

I clawed my way uphill through thick brush that fought every move I made. Often I would sink thigh-deep in small muddy pools. The strenuous effort plus the altitude and stress dragged me to the brink of exhaustion. *Don't let her be in here,* I prayed as I slogged ahead. *Please. Don't let her be in here.* Then my boot caught in the tangled brush, and I fell into a small pool of water maybe a foot and a half deep. I had run and shouted for over three hours. I struggled to get to my feet, but I could not move. My strength was completely gone. My voice was gone.

Trembling there on my hands and knees, I realized I had reached the end of myself. I couldn't go another step; I couldn't shout Jadyn's name one more time. I could only weep and pray in a hoarse whisper. "Dear God, I have nothing left. You can have my career—You can have it. Take my savings. Take my house. Take my airplane. Take all the stuff I have cherished." My voice gave out completely so that my final plea was a silent one. *Lord, I cherish this little girl more than all my possessions. If need be, take my life. Take me. But please bring this baby back.*

ANGELS ARE NOT STRANGERS

It was just a day trip for the young couple, a day devoted to hiking the majestic Collegiate Peaks. As they slowly made their way along an old mining road near the timber line, the forest began to thin, allowing them wider glimpses of rugged beauty—the kind of beauty that stifles conversation and makes man seem small—and a child almost invisible.

They might have missed her except for the hot pink T-shirt that stood out in stark contrast to the earthy greens, browns, and grays of the Colorado high country. They might have missed her if she had chosen to sit in the shade of the thick buck brush that blankets the region between tree line and jagged peaks. They might even have missed her if their eyes had been scanning the jagged rock sentinels that loomed in every direction. But that tiny splotch of bubble-gum pink caught their eye.

Investigation revealed that the splotch of pink had long blonde hair and wore fancy tennis shoes. Then they saw the innocent, fear-filled blue eyes that matched the color of the sky. Eyes rimmed with tears held back to maintain a facade of bravery. Eyes that revealed the soul of a little girl not yet ready to trust her rescuers.

"Are you okay?" the woman asked gently.

"I can't talk to you!"

"I'm not a stranger. My name is Molly. I'm a teacher."

"Well, okay then."

Now it was safe to let the tears flow, safe to take Molly's hand and, between sobs, blurt out the truth as she knew it.

"My grandpa is lost."

Indeed, grandpa was lost, and though he did not know it yet, he was in the process of being found. This moment, like a beacon, would help draw him back to life.

REUNION

I don't know how long I knelt helplessly in the water. Eventually I regained my footing and stumbled back to our campsite just in time to hear the radio on the forest ranger's belt crackle to life. "We have found Jadyn. She is alive and well."

I collapsed again, this time in grateful praise and thanksgiving. I was standing on the road when I heard the distant puttering sound of the rescue ATV approaching. There she was, blonde hair flying in the wind, riding shotgun in front of one of the volunteers. Our hero, Molly, had walked hand in hand with Jadyn down the mountain while her husband searched farther up for the family of a lost princess. As it turned out, the princess had walked almost two and a half miles straight uphill. They found her almost a mile above the spot where the rescue team had lined up to search for her . . . . downhill! Normal children may seek the easiest route. My grandkids are not normal children.

I remember one moment especially during the reunion because the rescue team later sent me a picture they had taken. In the picture I am crouching down to Jadyn's level, holding her hands. I didn't scold her. I didn't lecture her on the dangers of the wilderness. I remember the exact words I spoke to her. I memorized them.

In a raspy whisper, over and over I said, "I love you. I love you. I love you." Those are the only words that would come out of my mouth. They were the only words that mattered.

Thinking back, I also remember another sound—the sound of a stake driven gently but firmly into the ground, a stake anchoring this moment in my heart. Because even as I whispered, "I love you," it suddenly hit me: That's how God feels about me. That's how He feels when one of His children finally comes to Him after being lost. That's how He feels when one of His children steps from the wilderness of mediocrity onto the path of living fully alive!

Jadyn's rescue on the mountainside that day was not the end of a story; it was the beginning of one. Over the next several years I would discover other stakes that God had placed along the way, all of them pointing to the life my soul longed for.

My name is Ken Davis. I am Jadyn's grandpa. A year later I would return to the same spot to have one more stake driven in the ground, marking my life journey. But first I had some living to do. This is the story of how I found my way back to the path of living fully alive after years of wandering. I'm not a stranger; I'm not an expert; I'm a fellow traveler. And I fall down a lot.

I recently told a friend I was a little disappointed that it had taken me this long to follow the stakes and find the joy I experience today. I ended my whining diatribe with a sigh: "All those wasted years!" My friend leaned across the table and said, "Hey, you have today." What a profound wake-up call. That is all any of us have. Today.

Come with me to the land of the living.

Chapter Two

A WILD RIDE IN A
SHALLOW BATHTUB

THE ICY WIND STUNG MY FACE. TEARS POURED FROM MY eyes and froze as they streaked back along my cheeks. The bare trees lining the road became a flickering blur as I careened down the hill, picking up speed. I prayed silently, *Oh God, please don't let a UPS truck pull out in front of me.*

The entire family was celebrating Christmas at a cozy cabin in the mountains of Colorado. There's a two-mile stretch of road that runs past the cabin and down to the valley. When the snow gets packed by traffic and the temperature is just right, the road becomes perfect for sledding. On this day it was a little too perfect. It was a sheet of ice. I had bought several little plastic sleds shaped like shallow, miniature bathtubs. The hill doesn't look very steep, but when you're sitting in a flimsy little bathtub doing forty miles an hour, you get a very different perspective.

There's a loud crunching sound as the sled gets under way, slowly at first. Then as it gains momentum, the crunch becomes sort of a swoosh. The swoosh becomes a shriek as you reach speeds never intended for a bathtub. You steer by dragging one hand on the ice. Dragging the left hand produces a left turn and a very cold hand. Dragging the right hand turns you to the right. Dragging both hands doesn't slow the sled but produces gaping holes in your mittens. To brake, you tumble off the sled.

I blazed past my grandchildren, who looked like brightly colored sumo wrestlers bundled in their winter snowsuits. They had veered off into the soft snow on the shoulder of the road and lay immobilized in their overstuffed clothing. "Grandpa! Wait for me!" they hollered. No way! I take every opportunity to win a race, even if I'm competing against children. I shot down the hill like a one-man avalanche.

My heart was pounding, my face was numb, and endorphins raged through my bloodstream. Now at top speed, I screamed, "This absolutely rocks!" Then sky became ground and ground became sky. This repeated itself several times. Somehow I had lost control and cartwheeled at forty miles per hour into a snowbank. Snow was packed into every opening in my clothing. I was gasping for air, my wrist felt like it was broken, and a trickle of blood dripped from my nose. I remember shouting, "I'm alive!" As I wiped the blood from my nose and checked to see if my arms and legs were still attached, I was overwhelmed with a sense of joy. I thought, *Now this is more than just being alive. This is living fully alive, senses tingling, nothing held back!*

In that moment another prayer drifted from my soul: *Please, God, let me experience some of this in my real life!* I wanted this sense of adventure and vitality to permeate every facet of my being. My wrist throbbed as I dug icy snow out of my collar and my underwear. The crash reminded me that pain is a sign of life. You are going to get a lot more banged up living life to the fullest than you ever will sitting on the couch trying to decide, as Dave

Barry once said, "whether to open a second bag of potato chips or simply eat the onion dip right out of the tub."[1]

THE DESIRE TO LIVE

The second-century bishop and theologian Saint Irenaeus wrote, "God's glory is the earth creature made fully and eternally alive with the life of the Spirit."[2] Plainly said, the glory of God is man fully alive. In that defining moment, collapsed there in the snow—numb, aching, bleeding, surrounded by chattering, sugar-charged grandchildren—I felt *fully* alive. I was savoring a little taste of what God intended for my whole life. Not safe, comfortable, passive, and predictable, but *crazy*—filled to over-flowing with adventure, risk, and emotion. I didn't see Him do it, but God drove a small stake in the snow at the edge of the road that day. It was a marker of sorts that would later line up with other markers—stakes defining the path that leads to living fully alive.

This idea of living fully alive is not some thrill-seeking quest. It doesn't require leaping from an airplane or riding bicycles at breakneck speeds or jumping a log cabin on skis. I've done all that. What I longed for was to experience that sense of adventure in my everyday life. Shouldn't we feel some of the excitement that comes from jumping off a fifty-foot cliff into the water when we jump out of bed to live as God intended?

I SEE DEAD PEOPLE

Unfortunately that is not the kind of life we often experience. There is a misquotation often attributed to Henry David Thoreau:

"Most men lead lives of quiet desperation and go to the grave with the song still in them." If he didn't say that, he should have! What a contrast to what I felt on the sled ride. What a tragedy to think anyone would die without having really lived. But it was true in Thoreau's time, and it's still true today. Especially as we get older, most of us stop looking for new experiences. We stop living and start coasting. We become fearful of taking risks. We start *getting* old instead of *growing* old. There is a big difference.

When emergency medical technicians come upon an accident, they go through a specific routine looking for signs of life. Is there a pulse? Is the person breathing? Is the person moving? Is there light in the person's eyes? We even assess the health of plants by asking: Is it still growing? Is it vibrant with color? Does it still blossom? Does it produce fruit?

If you look carefully, you will find people all around you who show few signs of life. They haven't flatlined yet, but they stopped singing long ago. Rarely do their hearts race in excitement over the possibilities held by a new day. They lurch through the darkness like zombies, clinging to memories of what life used to be. But deep inside they long to live again.

You can find them in high schools, retirement homes, corporate offices, and church pews; and sometimes they stare back at you in the mirror. They are not what the little boy named Cole saw in the movie *The Sixth Sense*. He saw *dead* dead people. I am talking about people who are alive but living as if they are dead. People who are fading physically, socially, emotionally, and spiritually. Even though they have many years of life ahead of them, they are unplugging their own life-support systems. I see it in their eyes, hear it in their questions, and sense it in their body language. I see it in the way they have neglected their health. I hear it in their confessions of a desire to live again. As I travel the world telling this story, I am often surrounded by people who freely admit the fire in their lives is gone and who desperately want it to be reignited.

Does any of this sound familiar? Are you longing to sing your song but the music won't come?

Do you wistfully remember when every day felt like an empty page and you could hardly wait to write the next chapter?

Do you remember when you hated to go to bed because you might miss something?

Do you wonder if it's possible to recapture that creative spirit that kept you learning and trying new things?

Has tragedy stolen the joy from your life and frozen you in time?

Do you regret allowing your physical condition to deteriorate and wonder if you might ever regain the energy you once had?

Do you watch a child playing and feel a tug in your soul that makes you ask, "What happened to that part of me? How did that innocent exuberance disappear?"

Have you lost the joy of your salvation? Do you want to mount up like an eagle and soar once again?

When did we stop living life and start letting life happen to us? Sometimes busyness drains the lifeblood from our souls. Sometimes we disconnect from the Creator of life, and that marks the beginning of mediocrity. I refuse to stop living. At my funeral I want to hear these words: "I saw him move. He's alive!"

I, too, lurched through life like a zombie. I had developed a successful career and was rounding third toward home plate. Instead of living, I think I had decided to hang on to what I had. I slid before I got to home. Then I lay down waiting for . . . what? The innovative, successful track I had followed became a rut and now threatened to become a grave. Then I began to examine the stakes God had placed at strategic times along the way and began the journey I share in these pages.

Today at age sixty-five my life is as fulfilling, exciting, and rewarding as any time I can remember. I'm more physically fit and spiritually alive than I was at thirty-five. I hope that sharing this story will help you recognize the stakes God has driven in your life that can lead you to live fully alive, examine the status of your life, and give you the opportunity to sing again . . . lustily, loudly, and with childlike abandon so the whole world will hear.

Evidently I'm not the only one who wants to live fully alive. It starts at the beginning of life. When my first daughter was born, she was blue and still. The room was eerily quiet and peaceful. Then the doctors exploded into action. They vigorously rubbed her tiny body with towels and ventilated her with pure oxygen. Suddenly her face flushed a bright red and she began to scream, her arms and legs flying in every direction. It was no longer quiet or peaceful. There was pain, chaos, blood, exhaustion, and joyful exhilaration. She was alive!

In the song "I Wanna Feel Something," Trace Adkins sings of a yearning for something "that moves me, that proves to me I'm still alive."[3] A powerful line in Switchfoot's song "Awakening" says, "I wanna know that my heart's still beating."[4]

Two thousand years ago, the apostle Paul weighed in on the matter of living fully alive. He expressed his desire to live to the greatest extreme possible. His words are an anchor of inspiration to me. He said, "I want to know Christ and the power of his resurrection" (Phil. 3:10). Whoa! What could be more out there, more exciting and fulfilling, than experiencing the same kind of power that raised Christ from the dead? I want a piece of that action! Paul wasn't only talking about being raised from the dead at the end of life; he was talking about knowing that power *now*. It is possible. And he explains how. His declaration will serve throughout this book as a template for living fully alive.

For now it is enough to know that the quest to live fully alive has existed from the beginning of time.

This impulse is so strong that people spend billions of dollars every year on drugs and diets and creams that claim to bring new life. Young people seek thrills by performing dangerous stunts and living risky lifestyles, hoping to taste whatever it might be that will make life worth living. What people often don't realize is that this passion for living is a "God thing."

I knew that, but I wasn't experiencing it. I had started to die before I died. Benjamin Franklin recognized this phenomenon. He is often credited with saying, "Many people die at twenty-five and aren't buried until they are seventy-five." Franklin himself was a shining exception to mediocre living. This amazing man helped draft the Declaration of Independence at seventy, invented bifocals at seventy-eight, and signed the United States Constitution at eighty-one, all during a time when average life expectancy was less than fifty years.

Part of my problem was that I had become comfortable with being comfortable. I couldn't wait to retire and live a life of leisure. My zest for living hadn't disappeared totally, though like a neglected campfire it was smoldering, almost extinguished. Where once there were blazing desire, spiritual growth, and physical vitality, there was now only a wisp of smoke amid dying embers. But therein lay the hope. There were still embers! If you are still breathing, there are still embers burning in your soul. If you are a physical mess but want to change, there are still embers. If you face depression, there are still embers waiting to be fanned by a fresh breeze to a blazing fire.

It reminds me of Billy Crystal's character Miracle Max in that classic movie *The Princess Bride*. Told that the young hero of the film is dead, Miracle Max knew better. According to Max, the hero is *mostly* dead, which is different from being *all* dead.

If someone is mostly dead, he's slightly alive. If someone is all dead, "there's usually only one thing you can do: go through his clothes and look for loose change."[5]

Though no one had taken the change from my pockets, I was heading into the best years of my life with my song still in me. I was mostly dead. That was not what I wanted, but doing something about it seemed like an impossible amount of work and would require more energy than I had or wanted to expend.

On the surface I was successful: traveling the world, speaking to huge audiences, and building financial security. But on the inside I was a mess: battling depression, feeling hopeless, and believing that the best years of my life might be over. Then I saw The Picture.

THE PICTURE

Every once in a while a glimpse of what is ahead changes the course of our lives forever. For me it was a glimpse of what was behind. People say a picture is worth a thousand words. To me this was a one-word picture, and that word was "Noooooo!" It wasn't a book or sermon or Bible verse that gave me the kick in the pants I needed. It wasn't a speech by some inspiring motivational guru. It was a photo of me and my granddaughter at the beach. There I stood, holding her hand, silhouetted in the sun. She looked like a little pixie. I looked like a walking manatee wearing a swimsuit and a green T-shirt that billowed in the breeze like a party tent. Do you remember Jabba the Hutt in *Star Wars*? I looked like Jabba the Condominium.

I could imagine people on the beach yelling, "Move! We want to see the ocean!" I didn't dare lie down for fear that environmentalists might mistake me for a beached whale and push me back in the water. In public I made jokes about how I looked, but the ugly truth was my physical state and appearance were outward evidence of inward decay. Perhaps it was laughter that let me look at a fact I had ignored before. The humorous metaphors were much less painful than the truth: physically, mentally, and spiritually, I was obese. If I didn't believe the mirror or the occasional unflattering photo, I should have believed life. Life was screaming the truth at every turn. I had high cholesterol. I was losing feeling in my feet. If a grandchild wanted to escape me, all she had to do was walk fast. My anxiety levels were off the charts. I often had to fight off waves of depression.

I had let my life slip. That picture yanked me from denial to reality. If the precious girl holding my hand had been fifty yards offshore and crying for help, I could not have helped her. I was physically incapable of saving her life. Little did I know that in a few years her survival *would* be in jeopardy, and I would use every ounce of strength I had in an effort to save her. That day on the beach a stake was driven into the sand. Another one was driven into my heart, and it would motivate me to take one of the most significant steps in my life.

No matter how old you are, no matter your past circumstances or physical condition, you can live fully alive starting today. It takes commitment and perseverance. There will be pain. But it can happen. I know it happened to me.

As I started the process, one of the biggest and most catalytic changes was physical. I was sixty pounds overweight and had no idea how losing that weight and getting into shape would profoundly affect my life. That beginning sparked in me the desire to fire up every other area of my life.

I had not been living fully alive for a long time, but I was ready to start. First I had to change some of the attitudes that had sucked the lifeblood from my veins.

Chapter Three

THE POWER CURVE

A WOMAN LOOKED OUT HER KITCHEN WINDOW AND SAW her German shepherd shaking the life out of the neighbor's pet rabbit. Her relationship with the neighbor was rocky, and she knew this certainly would make matters worse. She snatched a broom from the closet, ran outside, and beat on the dog until he dropped the rabbit. The little critter lay there motionless, covered with dog spit and extremely dead. After a quick glance to make sure no one was watching, she maneuvered the rabbit onto the end of her broom and brought it into the house. She dumped it in the bathtub, turned on the shower and rinsed the body until it was clean, then got her hair dryer and blew the rabbit dry. She dug out an old brush from the bottom of a drawer and combed the rabbit's fur until it looked pretty good. When the neighbor wasn't looking, the woman climbed over the fence and propped the rabbit up in its cage so she could never be blamed for its death.

About an hour later she heard terrifying screams coming from the neighbor's yard. She rushed outside, pretending she didn't know what had happened. The neighbor came running to the fence. All the color had drained from her face.

Feigning innocence the woman asked, "What's wrong? Why are you screaming?"

"Our rabbit died two days ago," the neighbor sobbed. "We buried him . . . and he's back!"

ATTITUDE AND ALTITUDE

You can't fake being fully alive. You can fool people for a while, but eventually they will know. And you can never fool yourself. Being alive is more than simply looking fluffed up and combed out on the outside. It's a matter of attitude. And that comes from the inside. This book is full of challenges that will have an impact on every facet of your life. Approaching those challenges with the right attitude is the first and most important step you can take. Your attitude will launch your dreams or bury them.

I love the word *attitude* in that context because of the parallel with my experience as a pilot. In aviation *attitude* describes the position of the airplane relative to the airflow over the wings. At certain attitudes the plane will fly, but at others it loses its lift and the plane becomes a rock with wings. Almost every situation you can get into with an airplane can be solved with altitude, attitude, and power. If your engine quits and you are high enough above the earth, adjust the attitude (position) by pointing the nose toward the ground, and the airplane will pick up speed and fly again, even without power. The two most important places for an airplane to have a good attitude are at takeoff and landing. That's when the plane is closest to the ground and there's the least amount of time to make a correction. If you maneuver an airplane into the wrong attitude at a very low altitude, you can get behind the power curve. At that point no amount of power will help. All you can do is hold on and wait for impact.

Just such a situation caused me to crash my airplane while landing in Alaska. I was very close to the ground with the engine at idle and the nose too high. In aviation, as in life, if you have your nose too high in the air, that's a bad attitude. The plane lost lift and began to sink, but all the power I could give it couldn't stop it from hitting the ground. I was behind the power curve. I walked away from that accident with a whole new understanding of the importance of attitude.

The metaphor carries over into real life. Our attitude is what determines whether we can fly and how high we can fly. Here are some principles that can keep you ahead of the power curve.

1. BANISH THE SPIRIT OF FEAR

Few things can short-circuit your effort to live fully alive as much as the fear of failure. This fear will affect your ability to get in shape physically and move forward in your life of faith; it will also negatively influence every relationship you have. I ought to know. I'm a recovering perfectionist, "one who fears failure." That doesn't mean I was ever perfect; it means I spent much of my time feeling miserable because nothing I did was perfect. I painted pictures no one ever saw; I wrote letters I never sent; I planned trips I never took. If I couldn't do it to perfection, I gave up, and I certainly wasn't willing to make any imperfect projects public. In my mind, imperfection was failure. In reality, imperfection is life.

I have a confession to make. I struggle with attitude more than almost anything else. Not only am I a perfectionist, but I tend to look at everything from the negative side first. When I'm speaking and someone leaves the room, my first thought is, *I wonder what I said wrong?* If a thousand people come to me after a presentation and say, "Your talk profoundly changed my life," I'll obsess over the one person who walked by without a word.

Another part of my challenge is that I am surrounded by people who seem to be positive all the time. Even though I know they can't be 100 percent positive every minute of the day, I want to be perceived as a positive person. I'm saying this so you'll know I don't have all the answers. It's a daily exercise for me to stay ahead of the power curve and keep the plane at the right attitude. (Fortunately for me, this is changing. I'll share that part of the journey later.)

G. K. Chesterton said, "Anything worth doing is worth doing badly."[1] Chesterton wasn't encouraging mediocrity; he was alerting his audience to an important truth: if you wait to do something until you can do it perfectly, you will *never* do it. Give it your best shot now. Learn from your mistakes, and then do it better the next time. That's called growth. If I still operated as a perfectionist, you would never see this page. Someone would find me slumped over the computer thirty years from now, unwilling to release the manuscript because it wasn't perfect yet. Somewhere in these pages you will discover that this isn't a perfect work. But it thrills me to know that someday a reader might write her own book, a man might take his first step of faith or find his way back to living fully alive because I did my best and then pulled the trigger to get it published. Perfection is a goal to pursue, not a requirement for living.

2. FAIL QUICKLY. GET IT OVER WITH!

"For God did not give us a spirit of timidity, but a spirit of power, of love and of self-discipline" (2 Tim. 1:7).

Fear is the culprit that gives birth to perfectionism. Fear of failure is like a vampire that sucks the lifeblood from anyone trying to live fully alive. It's time to pull up our big-boy pants and face the truth: we are going to fail. After hearing best-selling author and speaker Andy Andrews give a presentation on how to build a career, someone asked, "What if I fail?" With his trademark smile and infectious enthusiasm, Andy answered, "You will fail. Do it quickly!"

When NASA sends a rocket into space, it heads toward a target hundreds of thousands of miles away. The target and the route for getting there are plotted out in great detail, a perfect trajectory to take the payload to a specific spot. What an amazing accomplishment. This is something like you standing outside your home, throwing a dart, and hitting the bull's-eye of a dartboard in Siberia. Recently I was surprised to learn that the path of that rocket is not the flawless line that was plotted in the planning room. The rocket makes mistakes during the entire journey. As the rocket begins to stray from its course, a computer identifies the error and sends a command to make a correction. The rocket makes the correction and gets back on course. The journey to its precise target is literally a series of thousands of errors and corrections, an imperfect path to a perfect target. Imagine if the rocket got discouraged at the first deviation from course and quit trying or refused to obey the command that would bring it back on course. Then you'd have to duck because there'd be a wayward rocket landing somewhere far from its mark.

A paraphrase of the apostle Paul's words in Philippians 3:14 could read, "I haven't got it all together yet. I still get off course occasionally, but I want to know the right course, and I will keep pressing toward my target until I get there."

I remember playing an amazing game that came with my first computer. The computer asked me to think of an animal and write its name on a piece of paper. Then the game required that I enter the answers to a series of ten yes or no questions. At the end of the ten questions, and sometimes sooner, the computer would name the animal I'd been thinking of. After hours of trying to stump the computer, I thought of a wallaby. I answered all ten questions, and my computer screen flashed the message, "You are thinking of a kangaroo." Woo-hoo! I had just outwitted a computer. I jumped up and did a little victory jig. When I glanced back at the screen, there was another series of questions that required me to describe the difference between a wallaby and a kangaroo. Once I answered those questions, the computer never again made the same mistake. The computer didn't give up. It was programmed to learn from its mistakes, using the new data. We should be programmed the same way.

3. COUNT THE COST AND PAY UP!

Pain is part of the price of living. It was part of the price of that wild and wonderful sled ride I described in chapter 2. Love is painful. Relationships are painful. Failing is painful.

On the way to Norris Lake, where we vacation every summer with our six exceptional grandchildren, my youngest granddaughter, Jadyn, was bubbling with excitement. This would be the year she would learn to water-ski.

The night before her adventure, she drew me close and whispered, "Will I fall?"

I looked into those blue eyes and whispered back, "Yes, you will fall."

She laid her head on my chest and thought for a moment and then looked up at me. "Will it hurt?"

I couldn't lie. "Yes, it might hurt a little, but I promise it will be worth it. Falling and a little hurting is the way you learn to water-ski."

Silence.

Then the words I wanted to hear. "I can do it!"

And she did. I wish you could have seen the smile on her

face when she skied halfway around the lake. She overcame the two fears that keep us from exploring the adventures and opportunities God makes available to us every day. If you choose to move forward in your quest to live fully alive, you will fall, it will hurt . . . and it will be worth it. Be prepared to pay the price.

So as we look down the road that will lead you to lighten up and live, drop any idea that it will be a perfect journey. Perfectionism, fear, and impatience are all rooted in pride. You might as well swallow your pride now. You will fall. There will be pain. But the goal is worth the cost. Failure and pain are the entry fee for trying, the foundation for learning, the price—and proof—of living fully alive. The only people who don't fail and don't feel pain are people lying in an open box at the front of a church.

BITTER OR BETTER

Zig Ziglar was the first person I heard say that everything that happens to you in life has the potential of making you bitter or better. I could handle that statement until he added, "The choice is yours!"

What? I have to make a choice? Doesn't the severity of what happens to me determine whether I become bitter or better? Doesn't my past free me to blame circumstances or other people for my present attitudes and actions? Ouch!

But wait! There is good news. The fact that I have a choice also means that I don't have to be a victim. Responding with bitterness sometimes feels better for a little while. But bitter is never better. Bitterness eventually diminishes the person who nurtures it. I become brittle, an insensitive shell of what I really could be. Every day the events of life force me to choose. Bitter? Or better? Choosing both is not an option.

How ironic that bitterness has zero effect on its target but surely destroys the one who chooses to harbor it. A wise teacher once said that it's like drinking poison and waiting for the other person to die.

Thinking about this book has forced me to reevaluate my life. Not always a fun process. I must confess that my default, knee-jerk reaction still occasionally can lean toward bitter. But I am a free man now. Seeing the miracle in lives resolved to let go of bitterness is like watching a rose battered by hail recover and blossom into beauty again. I am inspired by the examples of courageous people who choose to be better and live fully alive in the face of incredible odds.

My wonderful friend Roger Mateer is one such person. Roger is one of those people who had every right to be bitter and give up on life. He had two strokes before he was three years old. He developed life-threatening blood clots that the doctors could remove only by taking three-fourths of the frontal lobe of his brain. The fact that Roger was also born with clubfeet and limited use of his right arm did not keep him from going to college; marrying Cindy, his wife; and choosing to raise a special-needs child.

Shortly after his forty-sixth birthday, Roger was deer hunting when he suddenly lost vision in his left eye and couldn't feel anything in his left arm. It appeared at first to be another stroke. Thinking back, he remembered being forgetful, stumbling, and dropping things. Or maybe it was the effects of the oxycodone, methadone, and Vicodin he took for chronic pain.

Later Roger was diagnosed with early onset dementia and a life expectancy of four to eight years. He decided to outlive his life expectancy just to irritate the people who gave the prognosis. Surgery and drugs have done little to help him, though that doesn't stop him from deer hunting and pursuing other adventures with the help of friends. Five years after the event, Roger is still going strong. So-called experts telling him his time is short is nothing new. Following his childhood strokes, doctors told his parents not to expect Roger to live past age five.

Before his dementia diagnosis Roger had a near-photographic memory. Today there are times when he can't pull up a simple word or the name of an object. All his life he'd had limited use of his right arm. Now the left arm doesn't work either. That all adds up to two bad arms, poor vision, limited mobility, an unreliable memory, and supposedly only a few years left of life.

Combine that with a bitter outlook, and you have someone sitting in a corner, who is waiting for the end—dead but not yet buried. On the other hand, add it to unshakable faith in God and a passion to live fully alive, and the result is a man who gives more and gets more out of life every day than many young, *healthy* people I know.

Roger's unquenchable spirit and sense of humor are an inspiration to everyone he meets. As the disease progresses, his sensory system plays tricks on him. When he drinks a cup of coffee in the morning, it can taste like anything from a hot dog to lemon rind. Mountain Dew tastes like a margarita. (I'll take two!) Roger says that, for him, mystery meat *really is* mystery meat. Many of his friends follow his writing as he picks a flavor of the day. One day he bit into a blueberry tart only to have his senses overwhelm him with the aroma of the blue sanitizing cakes in public restrooms. That flavor did not make the flavor-of-the-day cut. I have grown to love this man.

I asked Roger how this last round of physical problems affected his faith. His response was honest and without hesitation. "There are times when I get down," he confessed. "People are afraid to associate with me for fear my disease might be contagious. But my faith is stronger than it has ever been before.

"All of us need to trust God. People like me know it because we are forced to lean on God, but many of us don't. God has a sense of humor. If He didn't, He would have given this to somebody else. I see God in everything—a ray of sun touching the leaves or the thrill of helping my neighbor catch his wayward donkey." (That was one I had never thought of before.)

Roger laughed, and his mind took a detour. "A few nights ago I had a piece of meat stuck in my teeth. It was driving me nuts. Then I remembered that my teeth were in a cup in the bathroom."

Another burst of laughter and then, with laserlike focus, Roger summed up what makes him fully alive. "I am not dying with dementia," he said. "I am living with it."

When I listen to Roger, I remember that I have a few ailments that have inconvenienced my life. The nerves in my feet are dying, which means I can't run as fast as I once did. I can't remember where I put my car keys. I have two bags under my eyes that won't fit in the overhead bin on an airplane. But whenever I begin to list my woes, I think of people like Roger and the suffering that Christ went through to redeem my soul. And I choose to *live*.

Attitude determines action, and action determines accomplishment. Now that we're ahead of the power curve, let's climb to an altitude where we can see what's going to happen next.

Chapter Four

THE "WOW" PERSPECTIVE

LIVING FULLY ALIVE WILL CHALLENGE YOUR FAMILIAR, comfortable way of looking at the world and spur you on to find new perspectives on life. It's time to see them with new eyes.

When we took our youngest grandson Tyler to the mountains for the first time after he had learned to speak, we drove over Trout Creek Pass, where an incredible view of the Arkansas Valley and Collegiate Peaks stretched as far as we could see.

Tyler took one look and said, "Wow!"

I said, "Can you say *mountains*?" and he said, "Wow!"

His mother said, "Tyler, can you say *cow*?"

He said, "Cow."

"Tyler, can you say *horse*?"

He said, "Horse."

"Those are mountains. Can you say *mountains*?"

He answered, "Wow!"

While we were on vacation, I met a man who was an avid bow hunter. He used to take every opportunity to be in the mountains, scouting and hunting, but had stopped. Over coffee one day I asked him why. "It's lost its wow," he said.

For too many people life has lost its wow. The lights have gone out. When it comes to bow hunting, I don't know what would reignite my friend's passion for the sport. When it comes to living, it's the never-ending adventure of being a follower of Christ that keeps the wow in my life.

The wow of life lived fully alive is breathtaking. It can also be intimidating. You might hear yourself say, "Embracing all this is too much, too hard; it'll take too long," or "This looks too scary." Walking over unfamiliar ground, you feel yourself stumble and say, "I can't do this." The dream seems too far out of reach. Once again, it is a matter of adapting a new way of looking at the situation.

I just spent a week with Tyler, the *Wow!* guy. His answer to almost everything is an enthusiastic "Okay!"

"Want to climb a mountain?"

"Okay!"

"Want to ride the four-wheeler?"

"Okay!"

"Want to get a flu shot?" I couldn't find him for an hour. Evidently there are some exceptions.

One morning I caught him stumbling across our deck, looking through a pair of binoculars. He seemed very frustrated and had a hard time keeping his balance. He was looking through the binoculars backward. Try it. Even your feet will look like they are miles away. He was experiencing tunnel vision. I wish I'd captured the look on his face when I turned the binoculars around and he saw things close up, detailed, and reachable. You couldn't pry the binoculars out of his hands. He even watched TV with them.

To me that is a perfect illustration of our efforts to live fully alive. At first the goal looks far away and impossible. You can't see yourself getting there because of all the obstacles and the lack of clear details to help you overcome them.

Try a new way of looking at your situation: turn the binoculars around! Don't be afraid to study the detail of what lies between you and your goal. It may be physical limitations, financial worries, the fear of alienating someone, or that old bugaboo—fear of failure.

With your eyes glued to that goal, develop a strategy to overcome any obstacles and move forward. As Paul wrote in Philippians 3:14, "I press on toward the goal to win the prize for which God has called me heavenward in Christ Jesus." Press on! Replace distant negative thinking with aggressive close-up strategy.

A DIFFERENT DOOR

Backward binoculars are not alone in affecting your view of the world. If you've spent much time nibbling around at the edges of life instead of going all in, it's easy to develop tunnel vision. This is an enemy of life. As your world expands, you need to broaden your perspective. Take off the blinders; you may be surprised at what you see.

This lesson was brought home to me in dramatic fashion moments before I was to deliver a speech to the managers of a major corporation. I never speak from notes, but this time was an exception. I had jotted down several pages of points I wanted to remember. Ten minutes before I was supposed to start, I decided to go over my notes—and couldn't find them. I had left them upstairs in my room.

I sprinted to the elevator and punched the button for the ninth floor. I had to have those notes! Here I was, the high-priced guest speaker without his notes. It was now seven minutes until showtime. The elevator stopped, and I heard a sound like the door opening and felt the little shuddering movement elevator doors always make, but the door didn't budge. It was five minutes until I would be introduced downstairs to the sound of polite applause, which now would likely be followed by confused silence and people looking around wondering where I was.

A bad word formed in the back of my brain and without warning exploded from my mouth. I kicked the door. I wasn't trying to be destructive; I was only helping the maintenance people. A good kick might jar the door loose.

Suddenly the elevator was going up again. Now I was frantic. The elevator crawled to the fourteenth floor and stopped. Once again it offered all the sound effects and tremors that accompany an opening door, and again the door remained shut. I lost control. Three minutes were left for me to avoid public humiliation before the tycoons of the world! I yelled, "Someone call the front desk! The elevator door is stuck!"

A meek voice behind me said, "No, it isn't."

Every hair on my body stood at attention. I was on the elevator alone! I turned around to see where the voice had come from. This was one of those elevators with doors on both sides. The door behind me was open, and there were five people waiting to get on. They had just watched me make a scene, and now none of them wanted to get in that confined space with me. Who could blame them?

As it turned out, the meeting had run long, and I arrived at the ballroom in plenty of time for my speech. After I finished, a sweet, elderly woman drew me aside. "I was standing there waiting to get on when the elevator stopped the first time," she said with a wry smile. She shook her finger at me and chuckled, "That was a bad word!"

How often we go through life beating on one familiar door screaming, "Something is wrong! Let me through this door!" If we would just relax and turn around, there might be another door open for us. But people with tunnel vision never do that. They have their eyes on this one door—this is what it has to be.

I've been on this ride before. Many times I've stood kicking at one door, screaming because it wouldn't open, while at the same time failing to see open doors of opportunity all around me—doors leading to thrilling new destinations and experiences. I've had tunnel vision. I have expected things to be the way they have always been and in doing so have put unnecessary limitations on what I could see and do.

Your path to living fully alive may be at the back of the elevator, the side of the elevator, or even right through the roof. It may take more effort than you expect. You might even have to take the stairs. But it is never too late to open your eyes and look around to a broader view.

Making choices means making commitments, taking a position, risking failure. Your approach to the process will either move you forward or hold you back.

A NEW PERSPECTIVE

On a flight from Nashville to Charlotte, our carry-on luggage had been taken at the beginning of the flight and stored beneath the aircraft. When we landed, we were told to form a line on one side of the Jetway and our luggage would be delivered to a door near the entrance to the plane. Not a good plan, but they'd always done it that way. There was no *Wow!* in sight.

The line of passengers waiting for luggage stretched all the way through the Jetway and thirty feet into the terminal gate. Finally the baggage handlers began to deliver the bags to a tiny door in the Jetway at the front of the line. Chaos erupted. People at the back of the line were so far away they couldn't see the airplane, let alone see their bags being unceremoniously dumped in a pile up front. The Jetway was quickly jammed with people trying to spot their luggage or dig it out from beneath the pile.

Then one person with a brain, the one person with a new perspective, yelled, "Let's do this!"

He grabbed a bag and started walking through the Jetway toward the terminal. "Is this yours?" he asked as he made his way through the people jam. A woman squealed with delight as she spotted her bag, thanked the man, and headed for her connecting gate. "Somebody grab another one," the man barked. A woman picked up a bag and made her way up the Jetway until someone identified it and took it from her.

Wow! A system was in place. Each person at the front of the line took a bag and headed up the Jetway. A steady stream of bags was being claimed. Within a few minutes everyone had his or her luggage and the Jetway was clear.

In this upside-down world you have only two options. You can choose to stand helplessly, waiting for somebody else to take care of you, or you can analyze the situation and do something yourself. It might be radically out of your comfort zone. It might be a new perspective. There is a chance it might even be wrong. But taking the initiative to do something different is one path that leads to living fully alive.

LIFE'S MULTIPLE CHOICE

I was never a big fan of tests in high school or college. However, when I had to take a test, my preference was the multiple-choice variety because there were usually four possible answers: A, B, C, and D. So I had a 25 percent chance of getting the answer correct, even with a wild guess.

After graduation the testing doesn't stop. Life presents multiple-choice options every day. Physically, mentally, socially, and spiritually, we face challenges that demand a response. You can't cheat on these tests like the ones in school, where there was always one kid (never me!) who wrote the answers on the palm of his hand.

As you decide what your attitude or perspective should be, or when you make any other choice, here are several suggestions that might help.

First, clearly identify your choices and how they are different. This may take some homework, but it is better to invest the time now than make a bad decision later. The time spent digging for answers will seem like nothing compared with time spent chafing under the consequences of a choice hastily made.

Second, eliminate choices that compromise your integrity or divert you from your goal. Consider only options that are consistent with your core values and purpose.

Third—and most important when it comes to living fully alive—never choose D. In most multiple-choice tests, option D is "none of the above." This is the choice of inaction and indecision. In political polls option-D people are the pitiful souls who have "no opinion," people resigned to following and never leading. Option-D people continue to dump baggage through a tiny door at the front of the line because they've always done it that way.

Hello! I see *dead* people.

Those in the option-D crowd consider all the exercise plans that might bring health to their lives but choose "none of the above" and end up staying in bed. They decide that since none of the choices are perfect or hold a guarantee of success, they will do "none of the above" and allow years to slip by.

They end up never writing that book, talking to that girl, taking that step of faith, getting that degree, or living fully alive. When it comes to living healthy, being fulfilled, or making a difference in the world, they will experience none of the above.

Do some homework:

- List the physical, spiritual, and social goals you need to live fully alive.
- Write down the obstacles that seem to stand in your way.
- Before you go to bed, add specific steps you will take to start in the direction of living fully alive. Don't try to map out the entire journey, but take at least one step tomorrow. Look around you for open doors of opportunity you may have never noticed before.
- Pull the trigger. Choose. A, B, or C—but never D.

The next few chapters in this book deal with the physical aspects of living fully alive. But the principles are applicable to all aspects of life. I can testify that the physical change in my life had a powerful influence on my attitude and was an amazing catalyst to living fully alive spiritually, socially, and mentally. For me it was a first step, like waking up. Don't bypass this challenge. I would love for you to enjoy the benefits I have experienced as I came alive physically. Later in the book I will detail the even more important spiritual, social, and mental changes that took place—changes of the head and of the heart. So get ready for the physical challenge in the next chapter that, if you choose to accept it, can turn your life around. Yeah, I know you've heard it all before, but this book is designed to help you act on what you've heard and take the first steps toward living fully alive. Your changes may come in a different order, but for now your first step is to turn the page.

Chapter Five

BODY COUNTS

AFTER SEEING THE "NOOOOOO!" PHOTO TAKEN AT THE BEACH, I realized how much I had let my physical condition decay. Today much of America is in the same situation. According to the Centers for Disease Control and Prevention, one out of every three Americans is obese. Seventeen percent of children between the ages of two and nineteen—12.5 million kids—are obese.[1] The Get America Fit Foundation reports that the prevalence of child obesity in America has quadrupled in twenty-five years. Three-fourths of Americans do not get enough exercise, and a quarter of them get no exercise at all.[2]

I am astounded at how many Christians neglect their personal health to the detriment of every aspect of their lives. The Bible says the body is the temple of the Holy Spirit. If the Israelites had let the temple fall into the same disrepair we allow our bodies to experience, it's likely the entire structure would have collapsed.

Truth is, our health affects everything! Once I made the decision to improve my physical health, my desire to grow spiritually, my mental attitude, and my relationships with my family and friends all took a dramatic leap forward. I went from being unable to tie my shoes without gasping for air to running, biking, and playing competitive sports for hours. I went from being so lethargic I hesitated to stoop down to pick up a twenty-dollar bill to diving for the floor when a dime drops.

No matter what your age, you can feel better today than you have in years. To reach this goal, you don't have to be a winner on *The Biggest Loser*, hang around funny-smelling gyms, go on a tree bark diet, or run a six-minute mile. You can start one day at a time, one pound at a time, one step at a time.

By losing weight and staying fit, you can avoid incredible punishment on your heart, joints, and organs; eliminate curable diseases such as diabetes; and avoid heart disease altogether. Once you begin to get healthy again, you will ignite a passion for excellence in every area of your life.

A healthy body gives you the ability and stamina to keep moving ahead. It increases your mental sharpness and makes it possible for you to more effectively glorify God by living fully alive. I saw major changes in every facet of my life starting with the first ten pounds I lost. Now fifty pounds lighter, I once again have the strength and stamina to cavort with my grandchildren as I haven't been able to do for years.

Should you have a Noooooo! moment as I did, you definitely will be inspired to get started. But even without such a moment, knowing that the choice is really a matter of life or death should be the greatest motivation of all.

BEYOND VANITY

Of course I wanted to lose that manatee figure and improve my strength and endurance. But most of all I wanted to live again.

Let me clarify an important point here. This is not about looking good. I can guarantee that if your motivation is limited to fitting into a certain size dress, your goal is too small, and you are setting yourself up for failure, especially if you're a man.

Most of us set goals that are too small. Wearing a certain dress size, reaching a target weight, or looking buff isn't a goal big enough to sustain you for the rest of your life. If your goal is too small, then once you reach it, your commitment fades. As soon as the zipper zips, out come the potato chips!

Without a bigger goal you will never maintain that weight or continue to fit into the dress. Before you know it, you're sliding downhill, struggling to recapture the same hard-won ground again. Over time your weight will yo-yo up and down, resulting in even poorer health, greater lack of confidence, and deeper discouragement. Been there, done that.

Guys, if your only motivation is to look like Adonis and be on the cover of *Men's Health*, you may as well aim at getting into a size six dress. As Keelan Hastings said in his book *From Vanity to Health*, "Vanity is not part of the equation."[3] All of the previously mentioned goals are great intermediate targets, but the ultimate goal has to be worthy of a lifetime of commitment—one that will motivate you to live every day fully alive, healthy, vital, and capable of being all God created you to be.

When we were filming the theater release for *Fully Alive*, I announced that I had lost forty-seven pounds and felt better than I had in twenty-five years. Someone in the balcony yelled, "Show us your six-pack!" You know, six-pack, that stack of abdominal muscles below your rib cage that is supposed to look like . . . well, a six-pack, and not like a keg.

I'm sixty-five years old and in fairly good shape, but here are some facts about yours truly:

- I don't have a six-pack.
- I never will have a six-pack.
- It doesn't matter.

You don't need a six-pack to live fully alive. I once had a potbelly. Now I have what looks vaguely like venetian blinds. No one talks about this, but the skin of a sixty-five-year-old does not shrink and cling tightly to the new muscles living beneath. My skin is satisfied just to hang there like blinds and protect those muscles from the sun. So, no, I don't have a six-pack, but the body I have now serves me well and allows me to serve God well. I am healthy and happy and physically fit enough to do almost any activity I want.

There is much more to life than being physically fit, and I can't wait to tell you about it. But you will need stamina, a clear mind, and willpower to do those things. So first let's look at the big picture. Your body counts.

SHUFFLE OR DANCE

Because you've already adapted a great attitude and gained some altitude, you can see the big picture and realize that the process is not complicated. And I am living proof that it works. Some of my first inspiration came from recommendations in Chris Crowley and Henry S. Lodge's best-selling book *Younger Next Year*, whose subtitle especially attracted me: *Live Strong, Fit, and Sexy—Until You're 80 and Beyond*. Sounded like an excellent idea, and I figured accomplishing two out of the three wouldn't be bad.

Their book is filled with practical advice about improving your physical condition no matter how out of shape you are when you start. There's a lot of detail, but at the risk of oversimplifying, I will tell you that their message in a nutshell is this: Exercise for an hour a day. Start right now. Stop eating junk. And do it for the rest of your life. There you go![4]

Why are you still sitting here holding this book? Let's get going!

The hour-a-day part shouldn't scare you; it should make you get started. If you begin moving for an hour a day and eventually find a way to push yourself to the limit several times during that hour, your body will be reminded that it is still alive and will begin to produce the muscle and stamina needed to live.

Do not close this book! The recommendations of Crowley and Lodge were based on solid evidence—if you don't use your body you will lose it. I can still hear you mumbling, "An hour a day!" The truth is that past generations lived a lifestyle that required movement and exercise eight to ten hours a day. Physical activity was a natural part of work. Farming, producing goods, playing games—it was all physical activity. Today, much of our work and our entertainment is done sitting down. Families used to structure the day with three solid meals of organic, healthy foods. Today we snack all day and well into the night on highly processed junk proven to be detrimental to health. In short, it is our sedentary lifestyle and the junk we eat that have created so many health issues in our lives. We are trying to live fully alive while dragging the chains of our own destruction with us.

In recent research by the National Geographic Society and the National Institute on Aging, scientists interviewed some of the oldest and healthiest people on earth and observed where they live. Many of these people live healthy and active lives beyond the age of ninety, and an outrageous percentage of them are still going strong at one hundred. Here is one of the discoveries they made: none of the people in these cultures did daily exercise. No weight lifting. No jogging. Nada. Don't close the book! You see, they lived lifestyles where movement was a part of their everyday life. They didn't have to jog or put on spandex to lift weights. They were in motion from morning till night.[5] Movement is a sign of life. So if movement is not already a part of the structure of our lives, then it is important to structure movement into our lives. One of the questions asked about someone who has been seriously injured is, "Is she moving?" If the response is yes, there is hope for life.

Are you moving? If not, it's time to start.

Oh, wait. I hear another argument. My Christian friends often counter that the Bible says nothing about exercise. So why waste the energy? This attitude is evidenced by the number of obese people sitting in the pews and even standing in the pulpit. Church membership is down because we can't fit all of them in the building. I have a friend who knows he is overweight and unhealthy. He quotes the scripture about our bodies being temples of the Holy Spirit (1 Cor. 6:19). Then he turns in a circle, displaying his opulent body, and says, "I'm building a mega-church." He laughs, the audience laughs, and, yes, I laugh with my friend. But all of us know that the poor health that comes with the "megachurch" falls short of what honors God. So to my friends who point out that the Bible says nothing about exercise, I respond, "Life in Bible times was exercise. If anything, the people in those days needed to set aside time to be sedentary, time to rest."

I remember hearing the story of a teenage boy who came to his dad. "Can I have the keys to the car?" he asked. His dad answered, "Until you bring your grades up to a B average, start reading your Bible, and get your hair cut, you will not touch the keys to the car." The boy was quite dejected, but for the rest of the semester he worked very hard. When his report card came out, it showed all Bs. He ran home, handed the report card to his dad, recited the book of Romans from memory, and said, "Can I have the keys to the car now?" His dad said, "Your grades are excellent, and you memorized Romans word for word. But our agreement was that you also had to cut your hair." At this the young man protested, "But Dad, Jesus had long hair!"

"You're right; Jesus did have long hair," his dad said. "And He walked everywhere He went."

In today's technological culture it is possible to get up in the morning and sit at a computer terminal or push papers across a desk for eight hours, then come home and spend the evening watching television. Many times the greatest exercise we get during the day is chewing bad food.

Places to explore and games to play beckon us to come outside and live. Instead, we sit in a soft chair, eat potato chips and dip, drink soda or beer, and then wonder why we can barely get out of the chair when the phone rings. If you don't move, your body thinks it is dying. It begins to shut down. So I grabbed hold of the challenge given in *Younger Next Year*. I committed to an hour of exercise every day for the rest of my life.

Americans today tend to start to physically decline before they turn fifty. Crowley and Lodge say that regular, strenuous exercise will keep us all healthy until the end of our lives. According to their research, 70 percent of premature deaths are lifestyle related, and daily exercise would eliminate half of all disease in people over fifty.[6] I don't know about you, but the words *premature death* are not particularly attractive to me. I like *fully alive* a lot better.

Crowley and Lodge wrote, "Most Americans today will live into their mid-eighties, whether they're in great shape or shuffling around on a walker. . . . 'Normal aging' is intolerable and avoidable. You can skip most of it and grow old, not just gracefully, but with real joy."[7] You have a choice. Shuffle or dance! Get old or grow old with real joy! I chose the latter, and it changed my life so dramatically that I can't keep quiet about it. In other words, a body in motion tends to stay in motion. A body at rest tends to rest in peace. What do you choose?

Chapter Six

NO EXCUSES

I KNOW WHAT YOU'RE THINKING: "THIS ALL SOUNDS FINE in theory. I would love to be able to live fully alive, but there are good reasons why I can't." I have heard most of those reasons and have used some of them myself: "I'm too old." "I have a physical challenge." "I travel." "I'm trapped at home." "I don't have time." "I keep falling off the wagon." "I'm already beyond hope." If the goal is to be healthy, to live fully alive for a long time with the energy and stamina to glorify God with your life, then anything that stands in the way of that goal can't be good! It's not a reason; it's an excuse. Let me give you some encouragement by sharing the stories of three people who had really good reasons not to live fully alive but refused to use them as excuses. It isn't their physical appearance, stamina, or even fitness that inspires most. It's their spirit of persistence and commitment to living.

FIGHTING FOR FIRST
DOWN AT FIFTY-NINE

Mike Flynt was small for his age when he went out for junior high football. In rural Texas in the 1960s, football was the biggest thing going, and a boy's value on the football field too often determined his value everywhere else. Mike weighed barely one hundred pounds. "You're a runt," his father told him, then said he'd never make it in football. But Mike held on to his dream. His junior year he grew eight inches and gained almost fifty pounds. The next season, he played defensive back when Permian High School (the school in Odessa, Texas, that inspired *Friday Night Lights*) won its first state championship.

He played college ball at Sul Ross State University in Alpine, Texas. But at the beginning of his senior year in 1971, he was expelled for fighting. As a junior he'd been team captain and the number one tackler; the loss of his senior year was devastating.

He finished school by taking off-campus classes, became a successful strength-and-conditioning coach, and eventually invented the popular Powerbase Fitness portable exercise system. He was shooting the breeze with some former classmates one day in 2007 and mentioned how he still regretted missing his senior year of football.

One of them asked, "Why not do something about it?"

Once the thought was planted, he couldn't get it out of his head. Though he was still in excellent condition, the idea of playing college football again after a thirty-seven-year gap seemed impossible. But after he learned that he still had one year of eligibility left, Mike Flynt, a fifty-nine-year-old grandfather and card-carrying member of AARP, talked his wife, Eileen, into moving from Nashville back to the west Texas desert. When coach Jerry Larned found out what Flynt had in mind, he told him, "You're an idiot." Mike tried out anyway, made the team, and became the oldest active college football player in NCAA history. His best-selling book *The Senior* is the story of Mike's determination to live fully alive.[1]

I have met Mike Flynt and consider him a friend. There's a fire in his eyes that you only see in people who are living fully alive. That fire doesn't burn because at sixty-four he looks like he could throw everyone out the front window. It burns because throughout the week he's helping people of all ages live to their fullest potential.

"I'm too old" was no excuse for him, and it's no excuse for you. And if you think a fifty-nine-year-old playing college football is a testament to determination, another recent story tops even Mike Flynt's.

STILL RUNNING AFTER ONE HUNDRED YEARS

In the fall of 2011, more than 3,800 runners waited behind the starting line for the Toronto Marathon to get under way. Among the crowd of entrants massed near the waterfront, jogging in place to keep loose, was Fauja Singh, a slender man wearing a bright yellow turban. Above the thick beard that extended halfway down his chest, his eyes were dark and his skin was chalk white. The rest of his body was covered by a form-fitting running suit.

This competitor, born in India, had traveled from his home in London to run in what would be his eighth marathon. He already held several distance records for his age group, with the possibility of adding to that list before the day was over.

Another kind of honor had come his way as well. He was the proud recipient of a recent letter from Her Majesty Queen

Elizabeth II wishing him a very happy . . . one hundredth birthday.

Fauja Singh, born in 1911, was one hundred years old.

He ran his first marathon in 2000 at age eighty-nine. Singh finished the Toronto course in eight hours and twenty-five minutes, about three hours off his best time but still ahead of five runners in the field.[2] Unless you are 101 years old, "too old" is a rotten excuse.

Of course, most stories of overcoming physical obstacles to live fully alive are not nearly as high profile and dramatic as Mike Flynt's and Fauja Singh's. I have a tenacious and talented friend named Saralee Perel who proves that the quiet victories can be just as inspiring and that you don't have to be in perfect health to live fully alive.

FIGHTING THE ODDS

Saralee is an award-winning columnist, a prolific writer of both fiction and nonfiction. She woke up one morning to discover that somehow the nerves in her spinal cord had been damaged and her brain could no longer send the right signals for walking to her legs. Her doctors told her she'd never get any better. "Though certainly unintentional," she told me, "my doctors did take something very important away from me: hope."

Since these were four of the most respected neurologists in Boston, Saralee gave up any idea of walking without a cane. It would be "impossible," they assured her. Then a psychologist friend encouraged her to try to walk anyway. The suggestion made Saralee angry. The experts had spoken, and that was that.

"They could all have been wrong," her friend countered.

"They said there's nothing I can do!" Saralee fumed. "No

rehabilitation. No physical therapy. I'm not going to put effort into trying to walk and then be miserable when I fail."

Read that last sentence again. That's an excuse so many people use: What if I fail? I'm so glad my friend's counselor was persistent.

"Trying is never failure," her friend said. Saralee picks up the story.

"I'd get steaming mad at people like her. What did they know? They came out in droves. I heard various things I should try: a soy-based diet, massage, yoga, acupuncture, positive thinking. All of these well-meaning non-experts believed that traditional medical doctors do not know everything about human potential.

"However, there was a common denominator in my friends' advice. And that was the word *try*.

"What made me finally try? The answer is simpler than I'd have ever imagined. That day I tried walking on my own, I had simply said to myself, 'Why not?'"

The first time she tried it, Saralee went out to her backyard, put down her cane, and started walking. She made it forty-two yards. Today she walks five miles at a time.

Her husband found a tandem bike with the seats side by side. He could pedal while she enjoyed the outdoors again. He attached pedals on her side too. Recently he bought her a bicycle of her own.

"Sweetheart," she exclaimed, "you know I can't bike on my own."

"I know," her husband answered. "And you can't walk either. Then why does the pedometer I bought you have seventy-four miles on it?"

Saralee says, "I have resolved to open my obstinate mind and really listen to others, experts or not. This not only fosters my own sometimes-frail belief in my abilities; it fosters faith in miracles. . . . How do we find hope when hope seems impossible? Do we simply believe in our hearts, our minds, and our very souls that we can beat the odds?"

"Yes."

Her inspiration came in part from actor Christopher Reeve, star of the *Superman* movies, who was paralyzed from the neck down after being thrown from a horse. Reeve's doctors told him he would never walk again, and, in fact, he died years later without taking another step. But he never gave up, and he devoted the rest of his life to promoting spinal-cord research.

Of his work, Reeve said, "So many of our dreams at first seem impossible, then they seem improbable, and then, when we summon the will, they soon become inevitable. . . . When we have hope, we discover powers within ourselves we may have never known—the power to make sacrifices, to endure, to heal, and to love. Once we choose hope, everything is possible."[3]

Saralee has been a tireless supporter of the Christopher Reeve Foundation. She has written a novel, *Raw Nerves*, and her column and other writing continue to inspire people around the world. Her persistence and feisty spirit and willingness to try have truly inspired me.

THE BIGGEST LOSER

One of my inspirations to start exercising was watching the contestants on the hit television series *The Biggest Loser*. When I started, I needed to lose 60 pounds; some of them needed to lose 260 pounds. That's like losing an entire me plus one of my grandchildren. I admired their improved appearances, persistence, and discipline, but most of all I admired their hope.

On the show the first thing the trainers do is instill in the contestants the hope that their goal is possible: they *can* lose two hundred pounds or more. From the first moment, the biggest challenge for them—and for the rest of us—is not measured in pounds lost or calories avoided or miles run. It is measured in a belief that the goal is possible and worth the commitment to make it happen. As Henry Ford put it, "Whether you think you can or can't, you're right."[4] If the amazing people on *The Biggest Loser* can do it, if Mike, Fauja, and Saralee can do it, if I can do it . . . you can do it. Persistence, commitment, and hope lead to life. Obstacles and challenges simply make it more interesting.

Chapter Seven

MOVE

I TOLD YOU THAT THIS BOOK ISN'T AN EXERCISE OR DIET book. There is no reason for me to duplicate the many helpful, detailed books that have been written on the subject or the invaluable information you can find on the Internet. But just as someone pushed me to get started, I want to do the same for you. I don't want this book to be your "Noooooo!" moment. I want it to be your "Yeeesss!" moment. In the back of this book you will find a list of resources to help you choose the exercise program that is the best fit for you. Here's the bottom line: don't wait another day to begin experiencing the life-changing benefits of taking care of your body. Read this chapter, and if there is daylight left, start *moving* today.

So where do you start? Move whenever you can and to the fullest extent you can. The possibilities are endless. I spent a lot of time moaning, "I don't have the right equipment." But tell my friend Saralee, who is partially paralyzed and walks five miles each day, that you don't have the right equipment. Wasting months deciding which exercise products you should buy or which program you should follow is really nothing but a tempting excuse not to get started. If you are alive, you can start living fully alive today.

I'll give you the same advice I gave to a woman who told me her story after one of my presentations. I had just finished my Fully Alive talk, which included how exercise and a healthy diet had helped me feel better and regain my love of life.

BREATHE

The woman—I'll call her Sharon—was sitting in one of those electric scooters you see advertised on TV. She managed a smile when I shook her hand. She was obese and looked like she might be in her late thirties or early forties. "Were you in an accident?" I asked.

"No," she whispered as she wiped tears from her eyes.

I discovered that no doctor had prescribed the chair for her. She had decided to purchase the chair because walking made her breathe hard. She poured out a story of how she had gained weight after college and slowly had lost her fire for living. Now, the power chair that kept her from breathing hard had become her prison. After a long pause she said, "Can you help me?"

"No," I said, "I cannot help you." The words came out quickly, and at first I wanted to retract them.

But my answer was not meant to be cruel or glib. My time with Sharon would be very limited. There was no room for mincing words. This wonderful young woman needed someone to tell her the truth.

"I can't help you," I continued, "but the good news is that you can help yourself."

"How can I do that?" she asked.

"You can breathe hard," I answered. Her eyes widened in astonishment. It had never occurred to her to look at it that way. "Do you use this chair to get the mail?" I asked.

She told me one of the reasons she got the chair was that she had a long driveway and the walk to the mailbox made her breathe hard. "I use this chair for everything," she confessed.

I asked her to look into my eyes. "If your doctor says it is okay, get out of this chair, starting tomorrow, and walk to the mailbox. Walk to pick up your paper in the driveway. Walk out to take a picture of the flowers growing at the edge of your yard. Do it again the next day. If it takes you an hour, let it take an hour. You will find that breathing hard will eventually help you breathe more easily. One day you will get the mail, open the door to your house, and realize you just walked that distance and are not out of breath. Then it is time to walk a little faster and a little longer. Increase the time you walk by ten minutes each week, and soon you will be walking for an hour. Don't be afraid of breathing hard. If you're not breathing hard, go faster. Breathing hard is the whole idea."

I encouraged Sharon to walk away from home for thirty minutes and then walk back. I do almost all my exercise this way. If I simply walk around the block, invariably I will find an excuse to stop early. But if you walk or run or bike away from home for the thirty minutes, you are committed because there is only one way to get back. Before you know it you will be going farther and faster than you ever thought possible.

I challenged Sharon because she sincerely wanted to live. Our time together was almost over. I tapped her powder-blue scooter with all its cute stickers and convenient baskets. "Get out of the chair and start to live again. This chair is a ride to an early grave. I am so glad you want to live."

She wept openly, but in her eyes was a glimmer of hope I had not seen before. She acknowledged what she had secretly known all along. Unless she started to breathe, the electric power chair would become her "electric chair."

Although Sharon's situation was extreme, her attitude was not unique. Most of us are experts at avoiding anything that makes us move or breathe hard. We take the elevator rather than the stairs. When we have to walk somewhere, we shuffle along like zombies rather than walk at a brisk pace. We step onto the moving sidewalk and stop rather than walk an extra fifteen seconds. My friend Kenn Kington was leaving the upper floors of a department store in Atlanta when the escalator he was riding suddenly stopped moving. Dozens of people stood on the escalator grumbling as they waited for someone to fix the problem. Kenn finally yelled, "Walk!" and slowly the sheep began to move. How disappointing and over-whelming it must have been to be forced to walk *down* a flight of stairs. If it had been the up escalator, Kenn might still be trapped there today.

Starting now, look for ways to breathe. Choose the parking spot farthest from the store, and walk across the lot. Pick up your pace! You don't have to sprint, but put some pep in your step. Look alive!

If you don't already have an exercise plan in place, put the book down after you finish this chapter and plan a way to breathe hard for at least an hour, six days a week. This is your goal. Find a way to push yourself to breathe extra hard several times during that hour. Run, jog, walk, or even shuffle if you have to, but get that heart pumping. If at first you don't suc-ceed, keep trying until you do. If you fall behind, don't give up. Sink your teeth into this goal and hang on for dear life because life is exactly what it's all about.

HAVE FUN

Some of your exercise is going to fall into the category of hard work, so it is important to mix in activities you enjoy. For you it might be tennis or swimming or walking. I love riding bicycles, playing racquetball, and running. My wife enjoys aerobic dance. I doubted the value of this activity as exercise until she invited me to attend a session. My graceful moves must have impressed the class because they smiled a lot. I struggled to keep up, and the next day I could hardly move. Aerobic dance *is* exercise. I'll stick to racquetball.

Racquetball not only makes me breathe; it makes me gasp for air. When I first started, I would often have to stop to catch my breath. Those first attempts at being an athlete also taught me that the mind is capable of asking the body to do more than it can deliver. In one game I ran to return a screaming shot delivered by my evil son-in-law. As I approached the wall, I heard a warning go off in my brain: *Stop! Wall approaching! Wall approaching!* My unconditioned legs were incapable of stopping quickly. When I came to, I felt something on my nose. It was the floor. I had crashed into the wall and knocked myself unconscious. Luckily I wasn't seriously hurt and was back playing the next week. Today I often play for more than an hour without stopping, trying to beat opponents half my age, and my nose never touches the floor. I can stop, turn, jump, and do all those things you see on the extreme workout videos. I sweat like crazy, lose weight, keep in shape, and have fun at the same time. I can also beat several of the disgustingly fit young men who play with me.

When I first started playing, there were occasions when I would swing at the ball and miss it. Actually, that's a little misleading. There were occasions when I would swing at the ball and hit it. Those frequent misses brought stabbing pain to my shoulder. Now I hit most of the balls that come my way, and even when I miss, there is no pain. The healing power of exercise is amazing.

Swimming and weight training are my least favorite activities. But the effects they have on my joints and back are incredible. Where once I was constantly icing a sore back, today I can throw grandchildren into the air and occasionally catch them. This past summer I slalom water-skied with my children and grandchildren cheering me on. I struggle to find words to express the joy I felt in that moment.

Weight training is the most difficult and exhausting for me. I have to practice more self-discipline to continue weight training than any other form of exercise. However, this kind of exercise, called resistance training, is essential to any program. Muscle burns fat. Resistance training builds muscle. Do the math. The more muscle you build and maintain, the more fat you burn and the less you have to depend on pounding the pavement to keep that marvelous body functioning.

Resistance training can be accomplished with a variety of equipment or no equipment at all. Free weights are versatile and relatively inexpensive. They also give you feedback as to your progress. As you gain strength, you can lift heavier weights or at least lift the same weight more times. Your local gym will have a variety of equipment that will allow you to work the different muscles in your body. You can purchase most of those machines, but they can be pretty expensive—although no more so than a big flat-screen television. Between what you can buy and what is available in the gym, you can find something that will get you moving.

Travel used to be my excuse for not working out. Then I met Mike Flynt and started using his Powerbase Workout Program that incorporates a series of flexible bands with different degrees of resistance. Mike is a guy who trained men and women in the armed forces and played competitive football at fifty-nine. He knows what he's doing. Now I throw a set of Powerbase bands in my suitcase when I travel. Over a hundred people of all ages from my church work out regularly using this system and have had amazing results.

There are other exercises you can do that use your own body weight. Remember push-ups? And squats? Lest you think these are ineffective, do three sets of fifteen lunges, and if you can make it to the phone, tell me what you feel the next morning. You can even improvise with items you find around the house. Why do you think milk jugs come with handles? Right! So you can fill them with varying amounts of water and have your own personal set of weights. Don't laugh; I've done it. It works. It's not about equipment; it's about consistent effort that works all the muscles in your body.

Every time I play racquetball, I pass a swimming pool where elderly people are working out. These people could easily use the excuse that their joints won't handle exercise. But there they are, doing jumping jacks and squats and running in place, minimizing impact by using the water as resistance. I admire these people. Their laughter is an inspiration to me as I close the door to the little enclosed court where I will chase a ball for over an hour.

The gym, with its rhythmic sound of people running on treadmills and the clank of metal against metal, is another option. These mysterious dungeons smell like a cross between a Michelin tire and a moldy sock, and when you first see the young, fit bodies that populate them, you might feel a little intimidated. It's so unfair! But if you look closely, few of them are looking at the other people there. They are looking at themselves in the mirrors scattered throughout the building. So relax. You are invisible. At my age I am exceptionally invisible. If I didn't move, they would close down the building with me lying on a bench. So grab some weights and move. If you have a gym handy and can afford to join, do it. It will have everything you need to keep in shape, along with people who are trained to teach you how to use it.

A click on your computer will tell you where and how you can get what you need to get started. And I'm telling you that if you are breathing, have a body, and have permission from your doctor, you can start to live a healthier life now. Keep it simple; do a variety of activities, and choose at least some that you enjoy. There's just no excuse for not doing it.

I told you at the beginning of the book that I'm not an expert, but I'm going to share my journey. I got started slowly, just as you will. Then after reading *Younger Next Year*, I kicked it into high gear, and the results were amazing. Now, for at least one hour, I breathe hard four times a week as I run, swim, bike, or play a sport and twice a week as I do resistance workouts or weight training. Once a week I take a day off. Because of my crazy travel schedule, I occasionally miss a day or get the routine mixed up, but I refuse to give up.

Choose an activity that gets your heart pumping, find a friend or stranger who will compete with you, and most of all, have fun. A few additional notes:

- *Start easy.* Always warm up and stretch out those muscles before you begin. Push yourself, but don't overdo it. There is an ancient Greek word for overdoing it. It's called *injury!*
- *Do your workouts outside* whenever you can. And don't forget the sunscreen and any protective gear appropriate

for the climate. An hour of exercise in sunlight could be more beneficial for your mental health than any single, legal dose of medication you can take.

- *Don't give up.* Recently I took a seventeen-day trip to Australia. The round-trip flight took fifty hours, and I missed several days of structured exercise. The temptation to give up was strong. But I refused. If you fall off the wagon, get up and keep going. Living fully alive requires persistence.

Once you get started, the list of resources at the back of this book and information available on the Internet will help you design a detailed plan that will help you track your progress and be consistent. The important thing now is *move*! Breathe! Get started!

A RUNNING START

Using running as an example, here's the general structure I follow. You can use it as a pattern for any kind of exercise you choose.

Before I start, I stretch my calves and hamstrings and limber up my back. Then I press "start" on my stopwatch and walk briskly for the first five minutes to continue to warm up my muscles and get my heart pumping. This warm-up is essential to avoid injury. If I'm not wearing a heart monitor, I start running at a pace that makes me breathe hard but not so hard that I couldn't carry on a conversation. This is a pace I could keep up for quite a long time, but I don't.

After two minutes, I push the pace to the next level. Whatever you are doing, do it a little faster; push yourself a little harder for the next two minutes. At this point I'm breathing harder. I can feel my heart beating, and unless I am running in the Arctic, I start sweating a little. An accelerated heartbeat and sweat are symptoms of being alive. At this pace I am not a good conversationalist. After two minutes of this I surprise myself by running for one minute hard enough to make me want to slow down. Not a full-out sprint, but hard enough so that no conversation would be possible. I'm too busy breathing. When that minute is done, I slow down until my breathing would allow conversation; then I begin the process all over again. Somewhere toward the end of the first thirty minutes, I run for one minute as fast as I can. I use this pattern whether biking or swimming or even playing racquetball.

On that last sprint sometimes I'm forced to slow down before the minute is over. It doesn't matter. For at least thirty seconds I have expended myself. At the thirty-minute mark I turn back and run at a comfortable pace the rest of the way home. If you and I were running together, we could talk all the way back. The last five minutes I slow to a walk and am careful to stretch all my muscles before I hop in the shower. Working out in intervals like this is very good for your heart. The pattern also makes the hour go by much faster than if you merely ambled along the road for sixty minutes. Sometimes I will stay with the interval training for the entire hour rather than go back to the intermediate pace on the way home. Mix it up. Have fun.

If you have a heart monitor, you can very precisely compute the different heart rates to judge each level of your workout, but I want you to be able to start now. I had one friend tell me he couldn't start because he didn't have a watch. That may be the lamest excuse I've ever heard. Here's the hard truth. You don't have to do it perfectly; you just have to do it.

I can almost hear some of you. "I hate running!" or "I detest walking!" But you like living, don't you? If you don't like running or can't run, do something else. I ride my bicycle using the same pattern. Actually, the area near my home is a series of steep hills, so the landscape determines my pattern. One minute I'm gasping for breath, trying to make it to the top of the next hill; then I'm rewarded with a terrifying ride down the other side. Here's the secret: don't coast. Sure you're tired, and you still have fifteen minutes to go. Of course you could just walk home or call a friend to pick you up. But if you still have the energy to jog, don't walk. If you can still run, do it.

If you're playing tennis, don't shuffle around the court. Run after that ball that gets caught in the net or bounces out of the court and across the street. Hustle to the opposite side of the court when it's time to change. If you're playing golf, stay out of the electric cart. Carry your clubs or use a pull cart. Maybe you don't want to breathe hard because you're afraid it will hurt your score. You can take it easy and post a lower score, or you can breathe hard and live to play many more rounds. What's your choice? Remember this: the pros walk the entire course. Forget the score. You are *not* going to make the tour.

This summer I watched a man with no legs play a round of golf. He rode in a cart rigged to tow his pull cart behind it. He would drive up to the ball, then crawl from the cart back to his bag and select a club. He would crawl back up into the cart and, using an extension on the front seat, swing the club at the ball. The only difference between his golf game and mine is that he hit the ball straight every time. Imagine climbing in and out of a golf cart between eighty and one hundred times in four hours. He was smiling as he played. I don't know if he kept score. But I guarantee his smile wasn't about his score. He was living fully alive without legs better than some of the cursing, disgruntled perfectionists I had seen on the course that day.

When I stay in a hotel, I often ask for a room on the upper floors. Once I get my luggage up there I use the stairs until I check out. That way I get to breathe hard every time I go to my room. Breathing is a privilege, not a burden. Just ask someone who can't breathe.

Yard work and gardening done at an energetic pace are great exercises. Just as with running, you can vary the pace of your work so that you get the blood flowing. The most calories I ever burned in a single day happened when I spent the entire day splitting and stacking firewood for the winter. There was never a time during that day when I felt exhausted, yet I burned more than four thousand calories because I was lifting and moving all day. No wonder lumberjacks don't need treadmills.

On a larger scale, here's what an average week of exercise looks like for me. Starting with this, you can establish your own pattern. Remember to be flexible. Things that aren't flexible break easily. On Monday I challenge my son-in-law Scott to a game of racquetball. This game is filled with explosive, almost constant movement. It's good for your muscles and for your heart and lungs. The first time you play you might even see your lungs; that's how hard you will breathe. However, after a couple of weeks, an hour of racquetball leaves you feeling like you can conquer the world. Wait, I heard that! No! You are *not* too old! I play with guys in their seventies who can tear me to shreds on the court.

On Tuesday I ride my bike, not only because I love riding but because I like to put off running as long as possible. I ride over a series of hills and never cease to be thrilled with what happens to my spirit when I have covered fifteen or twenty miles in the sunshine. My heart soars when I am outside feeling the sun, the rain, or even the snow. Sometimes a deer will watch me with wide eyes as I pass by. I have seen a beautiful tom turkey strut his stuff as he challenged me for the attention of two unimpressed hens. I have seen wonderful evidences of life, foxes, opossums, and rattlesnakes. I have watched the sun rise and seen glorious sunsets. I have prayed and mulled over problems. I have listened to music, audio books, and motivational tapes. I have even reviewed some of the sermons that have inspired my life.

On Wednesday I do resistance training. Since I don't like to sweat with strangers, I bought a set of weights and a workout station that gives me a wide variety of workout options at home. The idea is to work all of your muscles and remind each of them they are still needed. Your body is still alive. So on Wednesday I remind my upper body, and on Friday I remind my lower body. If I am in a hotel that does not have a workout facility, I can get a great workout with just my briefcase and a sturdy chair. I also have those convenient Powerbase bands I can use anywhere.

Thursday I run. I have to be honest. I hate getting up to run. I hate the first ten minutes of running, but after that the endorphins kick in, and the time seems to fly by.

Friday I do weight training for my lower body, and on Saturday I pick something fun. I might take a longer, more leisurely bike ride to explore an area I have never seen or play a game of golf. I try to be creative and try new things; I might even swim for variety so that I never become bored.

On Sunday I plan nothing, but that doesn't mean I don't do anything. After church I sometimes play volleyball with friends or canoe down the Harpeth River. And yes, I might watch a football game. This is a day to rest and relax, but it still doesn't hurt to move.

The important thing is to have a plan, but keep it flexible. If on Monday you have the opportunity to play a game of tennis with an old friend, *do it*. Do it for two hours if you want. If you travel or if an emergency keeps you from doing your weight lifting in the morning and you find yourself settling into the easy chair before dinner, *don't do it.* Take a brisk walk or run or chop wood. Tear down the garage and rebuild it. Do something every day. Once you catch the bug of being active and once you feel the benefits to your body and soul, it's easier to make moving a priority. After the first week of consistent movement and breathing, you will feel a difference. All the old excuses and resistance will still be there, but a new desire to be fully alive will help you fight off the temptation to put your body in neutral and coast toward immobility.

I know you read somewhere that you don't need to move an hour a day or even six days a week to benefit from exercise. I heard you thinking that several chapters ago. But I will tell you that after sixty years of trying, it was the challenge to be *younger next year* and the commitment to move for an hour a day that changed my life. When I absolutely can't do the hour, I still benefit from whatever time I can devote to it. Get started. Aim for an hour a day, six days a week, for the rest of your life and kiss the manatee good-bye.

Chapter Eight

FROM POLE TO POLE

MY FIRST ATTEMPTS AT EXERCISE WERE SPORADIC, AND IT took me a while to learn what healthy eating was all about. I knew I didn't have the perfect plan, but it was gratifying to be headed in the right direction. I was anxious to address the spiritual and emotional areas of my life but realized that living up to my physical potential and maintaining a healthy lifestyle was critical if I wanted the energy to join the parade again. Eventually I developed a consistent strategy that I could follow for the rest of my life.

My doctor was thrilled when he heard my long-term plan, but he never asked what steps I would take to get there. Whether you're working toward living fully alive physically, mentally, socially, or spiritually, short-term goals and immediate action steps are essential if you expect any progress. It isn't enough just to make a plan; you have to work the plan. That's why those stakes we talked about earlier are so important. They're markers that will give you a glimpse of where you've come from. But you can also drive stakes in the future that will help you take the next steps leading to the ultimate goal.

Crowley and Lodge tell how the captain of a sailing ship kept moving ahead even when the ship was dead in the water because the wind had died. He ordered his crew to load a light anchor called a kedge into a longboat and row half a mile or so out in front of the ship. The longboat sailors set the anchor there, and everyone aboard ship pulled on the anchor line until the ship moved that half mile. Then they moved the kedge another half mile out and pulled on the line again. It was slow progress that carried a whiff of desperation, but it *was* progress and much more desirable than being dead in the water. It kept them motivated and moving forward until the wind picked up.[1]

My form of kedging was signing up to compete in a triathlon. That may seem like an unlikely and desperate goal for an out-of-shape, sixty-plus-year-old man, but I learned that if I expected to finish that race I would have to keep dividing the task into bite-size steps until the action was small enough to put on the calendar and accomplish. If I wanted to be at the top of the mountain, I would first have to step over the branch in front of me. I could do that. Then I would have to climb the ridge. I could do that. Next I'd have to cross the stream on the other side of the ridge. I could do that. With that kind of commitment, one day I would stand at the top and see a hundred miles in every direction.

When I get up in the morning, my mind tells me I can't run for an hour, and my aching body seconds the motion. But I can walk for a short distance. So I get up and head out the front door. Once I'm on my way, I tell myself that I might as well run for a little while. In the last chapter I talked about a pattern for interval training. You don't need a watch to do this. During my run, I often pick out a telephone pole or a road sign or some pathetic remnant of roadkill. That's my stake. My little kedge. I prepare my body and mind to run full speed to that marker. I choose a marker far enough away so that it's a challenge, but close enough so I won't kill myself trying. (By the way, "killing yourself" is just a figure of speech meaning, "I don't want to use up all my energy before the hour is over." If your doctor gives you thumbs-up, you can rest assured that strenuous exercise is not going to kill you. Your body will stop you from running long before you keel over.) How great it feels to sprint past the next telephone pole. That pole becomes the finish line for my imaginary marathon. I raise my arms in victory, acknowledging the cheers coming from the invisible throngs lining the road. Then I slow down, catch my breath, and choose yet another marker where I will once again set an intermediate pace for my run. That possum lying in the middle of the road is perfect. By varying the pace between poles, mailboxes, and possums, thirty minutes have passed before I know it, and I turn around and head for home. Running from pole to pole never seems daunting to me. I don't have to run six miles or sprint for an hour. I only have to make it to the next telephone pole.

The same idea works with other kinds of disciplines. My friend Steve is a recovering alcoholic. He called me one night in a panic. He was sitting in a distant hotel room, overcome with the temptation to go down to the bar and have a drink, but he'd been down that road enough times to know that it was a dead end. For Steve there was no such thing as one drink. If he gave in to this temptation, his record of sobriety would be broken, his confidence would be shaken, and his family and career could be at stake. "I don't know if I can do this the rest of my life," he confessed.

I identify with Steve even though I'm not an alcoholic. We all face decisive moments like this on the battlefields of life. I could only give Steve some advice that had served me well in times of spiritual combat.

"Steve, you don't have to resist for the rest of your life," I said. "You need only to resist tonight. Don't drink tonight. Tomorrow is another day, and you can face tomorrow when it comes." Steve didn't have to run a marathon; he just had to make it to the next telephone pole. "Take it one day at a time," I told my friend. When he woke up the next morning, the overwhelming desire for a drink was gone. Steve said, "I *can* do this for the rest of my life, one night at a time." He has thanked me many times for the encouragement I gave him that night.

If you are seeking to develop spirituality in your life, pick out a telephone pole. Find that Bible you haven't read for a while. That's one step. Choose a study guide to follow. That's another step. Set a time for reading, prayer, and meditation. It won't happen all at once, but no matter what aspect of living fully alive you are striving for, you can break that goal down into manageable chunks.

One of my favorite examples of how taking small steps can make even the most impossible task seem possible is a story Anne Lamott tells in her wonderful book *Bird by Bird*.

Thirty years ago, my older brother, who was ten years old at the time, was trying to get a report on birds written that he'd had three months to write, which was due the next day.

We were out at our family cabin in Bolinas, and he was at the kitchen table close to tears, surrounded by binder paper and pencils and unopened books on birds, immobilized by the hugeness of the task ahead. Then my father sat down beside him, put his arm around my brother's shoulder, and said, "Bird by bird, buddy. Just take it bird by bird."[2]

There you go. You don't have to run for hours or years. You don't have to write a whole book at once; you can write it "bird by bird." You don't have to read the entire Bible in one sitting; you only need to get to the next chapter. You don't have to be the perfect mother or father by tomorrow; take the time today to say, "I love you" and encourage your child. As Paul said, "Keep pressing toward the mark." And you don't have to exercise every day of your life. You only have to do it today. Facing challenges and lofty goals with that strategy in mind makes them doable. One telephone pole at a time, one day at a time, one decision at a time—making progress on the road to living fully alive.

That's why I chose to compete in the triathlon. It was a *big* telephone pole on the horizon that would take me closer to being the man I wanted to be. It was my big kedge! I wanted to get below two hundred pounds and improve the state of my body, mind, and spirit. So I dragged the anchor out six months in front of me and signed up to compete in the triathlon. The manatee decided to go for the gold! For some of you this may not seem like a fun goal, but for me it was an exciting challenge that would keep me focused and on track. Winning wasn't the point. I didn't intend to compete against anyone but myself. Still, I had to get in good enough shape to finish the race, so I started training right away.

TRAINING FOR THE TRIATHLON

The triathlon I signed up for was an entry-level competition called a Sprint. To compete I had to swim (survive) for two hundred meters, bike eleven miles, and run two miles. Exercising for the rest of my life was not something I wanted to think about, but preparing for a triathlon with some friends was an exciting adventure that required vigorous training. I could do that.

I went from sporadic training to pushing myself hard every day, six days a week. I signed on with an Olympic champion to teach me how to swim fast. She and I learned quickly that I would never swim fast. For me, swimming is more a survival technique than an exercise. My main goal is not speed; it's staying off the bottom of the pool. But my persistence did increase my speed. I still can't swim fast, but I can swim faster.

At first it was agony. My joints screamed for my body to send some oil. Eventually they got the oil they needed, and today my shoulders are free of pain. Yet another reminder: use it or lose it.

Bicycling became my favorite exercise. I hadn't ridden a bike for close to ten years, so it took time to build my strength and endurance. The first day I rode, I woke up full of energy and expectation, climbed on the bike, got on the two-lane country road outside my house in Tennessee, and headed up the grade I have since named Yardstick Hill.

My plan was to time how long it took me to get to the top of the hill, then measure improvement from one day to the next. Only I didn't make it to the top that first day. I didn't even make it halfway before I had to stop. I stood there straddling the bike, gasping for breath, arms jellified, thighs screaming for mercy. I took a short rest, summoned all my strength, lifted my cell phone to my ear, and called my wife to come get me.

I remember the first time I committed to run for an hour. It was a hot September afternoon when I set off at a pretty good pace. My feet were sore, my back hurt, and I was sweating profusely. After thirty minutes I decided to change my pace. I sat at the edge of the road and called Diane to come get me. This happened three times before she gave me the following pep talk. "Ken," she said, "I'm not coming to get you again. If you can't ride up this hill, walk. If you can't walk up this hill, crawl. If you can't do either, rest until you can. Don't call me unless you pass away." Then she added the words that built a fire in me. "I know you can do this."

Shortly thereafter I started running and actually enjoying it. I followed Diane's advice. If I couldn't run anymore, I walked. Usually after a few minutes of walking I'd feel good enough to run again. Soon I was running for the full hour. Then I began sprinting between some of the telephone poles. I marked off a two-mile stretch of road and once a week would start my run on that stretch, competing against the best time I had posted before. I started losing weight and gaining energy.

OVER THE FINISH LINE

The day of the triathlon was such a milestone. Five friends raced with me. One friend, Mike, had trained with us after recovering from surgery. Although he couldn't compete that day, he had lost thirty pounds training for the race and was feeling better than he had in years.

The triathlon started in the pool. I swam faster than I ever had before, though not fast enough to catch my young friends who cut through the water like playful dolphins. If you have any doubts about my speed, I have one friend who waded on the bottom of the pool most of the way and still posted a better swim time than mine. I could see his backside moving ahead of me during the entire swim. It was infuriating.

After the swim I "spraggered"—a combination of sprinted and staggered—toward the transition area where my bike was waiting. I knelt beside the bike to slip on my biking shoes and helmet, lost my balance, and knocked several bikes from their racks—not exactly the image of athletic prowess. Finally I was on my way. The wind felt so invigorating as the water evaporated from my body. My heart soared. I was passing people. The manatee was passing people! Ten minutes into the race I saw my young dolphin friends riding up the hill ahead of me. I picked out a telephone pole at the top of the hill, stood up in the pedals, and cranked full out. "Here he comes!" I heard one of them yell to his buddy. They tried to stay ahead of me, but it was too late, and I was too fired up. I breezed past them all, and as I passed the telephone pole at the top of the hill, I whooped in joy. My heart was pounding as I savored the downhill opportunity to catch my breath.

The transition from biking to running went smoothly. I didn't tip over. The race ended much too soon. I sprinted across the finish line feeling . . . fully alive!

As we celebrated after the race, my friends and family excitedly pulled me to the tent where the awards were being given out. I had placed second in my age group (and yes, there were more than two people in my group!). I had never received an athletic award in my life. I was overwhelmed with joy. I later discovered that I not only placed second in my group but also finished with a better time than almost half of all the competitors!

As exciting as that was, it didn't matter. Life doesn't have a winner's circle; it has a finish line. And the only way to make it to the finish line is to take the next step.

PACE YOURSELF

Perfectionists are an impatient bunch. They conclude, "I don't have time to wait for the changes that need to happen in my life, so I'll double down on everything and be a totally new person tomorrow." If that's your tendency, you're going to hate my next bit of advice. Whether you are looking to strengthen your body, your faith, or your relationships, you will need to pace yourself. If you try to go too fast or do it all at once, you are setting yourself up for an avalanche of unnecessary pain and disappointment.

From a very early age, perfectionism has gotten me in trouble. When I was on the high school track team, I signed up to compete in an 800-meter run, which is about half a mile. So I marked off a half-mile route that wound through the pastures and back roads of our farm. Every day I ran as cud-chewing, rheumy-eyed cows watched me dodge their droppings. The day of the big track meet I was ready to go. This was a special day because my girlfriend was in the stands. She didn't know she was my girlfriend, but I knew. I thought that maybe winning this race would win her heart. So my plan was to start strong, get in front, and stay there until I crossed the finish line. I would run the perfect race.

When the starting gun fired, I took off like a shot. After the first turn I was in the lead. Then one by one, runners began to pass me. By the time I reached the halfway point, I was out of gas. I tried to keep going, but my legs voted against it. My stomach also rebelled. Evidently the sandwich I had eaten earlier in the day did not want to run with me anymore. Before I knew it, I was kneeling on the infield grass. The sandwich came up first, followed by a grape I had eaten when I was seven.

My "girlfriend" was not impressed. I left the stadium in defeat without finishing the race.

That experience taught me two lessons. First, pace yourself. Life isn't a hundred-yard dash; it's a marathon. The prize goes to the one who finishes well, not to the one who is first out of the blocks. Second, don't give up. My biggest regret is not that I created a grape spectacle but that I didn't finish. Runner and philosopher George Sheehan reportedly said, "It's very hard in the beginning to understand that the whole idea is not to beat the other runners. Eventually you learn that the competition is against the little voice inside you that wants you to quit."

My inability to pace myself cost me my lunch and any chance I had of impressing the girl of my dreams. Most of all it cost me the chance to finish well. As you read the challenges in this book, you will be tempted to try to do it all at once. You will be tempted to get results before you go to bed. Relax. In order to make significant gains you will need to push yourself, but don't punish yourself.

When I first started lifting weights as part of my manatee eradication plan, I found a best-selling book by Bill Phillips titled *Body for Life*. Inside were photos of people who had developed from scrawny wimps to muscular superheroes in ninety days.[3] The pictures reminded me of the old Charles Atlas comic book ads showing a ninety-eight-pound weakling getting sand kicked in his face in one frame, then the same guy massively muscle-bound and surrounded by pretty girls in the next.

Body for Life gave a very effective formula for weight lifting. I had a philosophy that if a little is good, a lot is better. So I took the formula and revved it up. I started by pressing a barbell loaded with 150 pounds of weights over my head until I couldn't lift it anymore. I called for my wife, Diane. "Take ten pounds off each side," I begged. She removed twenty pounds, but it didn't feel much different. I lifted what was left maybe twice, then said, "Take off some more." She kept taking off more weight, and after each time I would lift what was left until I couldn't lift it anymore.

Finally I had her remove all the weights and lifted just the bar until I couldn't lift that anymore. "Take the bar away," I gasped. Thinking I would be able to take a picture of my newly bulging biceps the next day, I decided to go all the way. I lifted only my hands above my head until I couldn't do it another time. I was exhausted, but, boy, was I nailing this weight-training program!

Diane said, "Look at you." I looked down, and the veins in my arms were bigger than my legs, my muscles engorged with blood. I looked back at my wife and thought I saw a twinkle in her eye as she said, "Go take a shower." Was this an invitation to romance? I got in the shower. It felt so good having the soothing hot water run over me. I put some shampoo in my hand, and then I just stood there. I was so weak that I couldn't get my hand up to my head. Mr. Muscle Man couldn't lift a glob of shampoo. I had just guaranteed at least four or five days when I wouldn't be able to do much of anything. I eventually squirted the shampoo on the shower floor, knelt down, and rubbed my head in it.

As you begin the journey to living fully alive, even as you make attitude adjustments, look for balance, and pace yourself. If you lift weights until you collapse or try overnight to make every change in your life that needs to be made, you will end up lying in a discouraged heap with a glob of shampoo in your hand. Pushing yourself without punishing yourself is a balancing act well worth the effort. Remember that the race will continue tomorrow.

When you skip workouts for several days because of travel or tragedy or just because you fell off the wagon, don't try to start where you left off. Ease into your weight training with lighter weights and work back to where you were. Run or bike slower the first couple of times out. Play a more relaxed game of tennis or racquetball. Remember that consistency is much more important than intensity.

CALL IT A DAY

In a treadmill world there is another part of pacing you must not forget. Take time to rest. God offers moments of respite and peace for your soul. Rest is an important part of pacing yourself. Studies show that the people who live the longest on earth are those who take advantage of a day of rest. Perhaps the reason God asked us to keep the Sabbath day holy and rest on that day is because He wanted us to live. People who have difficulty resting or suffer with insomnia are deprived of many of the joys of living. Peak performance demands that you take time to rest. God Himself set the example for us.

It was creation. God and an angel were sitting on the edge of the universe, enjoying the scenery. God took a deep breath and said, "I just made a twenty-four-hour period. Half of the time it will be dark and the other half, light. This will be a seven-day cycle that will keep repeating itself until the end of all time."

"Wow," the angel said. "What are You going to do next?"

God thought for a minute and said, "Well, I'm tired. I think I'll call it a day."

Years ago darkness would drive people from the fields. They would come home, take a bath, and spend the evening with the family. They could not bring the field, the cows, or the chickens into the house. They called it a day. Men and women would come home from work. They couldn't drag the office with them on some electronic device. There were no devices. They turned out the lights at the office, locked the doors, and came home. They called it a day. Today we bring the office and the field and the chickens and the cows and the worries of life into the sanctuary of our home. We drag them on iPads and smartphones, to the table and into our bathrooms and bedrooms. No wonder we're so exhausted.

Thus the heavens and the earth were completed in all their vast array.

By the seventh day God had finished the work he had been doing; so on the seventh day he rested from all his work. And God blessed the seventh day and made it holy, because on it he rested from all the work of creating that he had done. (Genesis 2:1–3)

Imitate the Creator of all things. Once a week, call it a day.

ONE STEP AT A TIME

Danny de Armas is a gifted leader and dreamer. He was one of the people who believed in me and spent seven years as a valuable member of my team. In 2009, he and I spent a week bowhunting in the rugged Collegiate Peaks of Colorado. One day after hiking and hunting all day, we began the final three-mile hike back to our base camp. Three miles on flat ground is nothing. Three miles in rugged mountains with a fifty-pound pack is a major challenge. Especially since we were now staring at the final 12,900-foot ridge we had to climb to make it to camp. We had been on the move since four a.m. It seemed that with each foot gained in elevation my pack grew heavier and my legs grew weaker. The only sounds were our gasps for air and the crunch of our boots.

Then another sound made me look up. It was distant thunder. Black, menacing storm clouds were flexing their muscles in the west. Could we beat the storm that was obviously moving our way? It was an important question. The last thing we wanted was to be caught on the top of a treeless ridge with lightning stomping around us looking for the easiest route to the ground. Three-quarters of the way up the ridge, it became clear that this was going to be a close race. No one wanted it to end in a tie. Although the sun was still beating down on us, the clouds grew darker and closer as we watched snaky tongues of lightning searching the ridges for us. Now, I was breathing in huge rasping gasps.

Finally I stopped and turned to Danny. "I don't think I can make it. How are we ever going to get to the top?"

Without stopping, Danny replied with determination, "One step at a time, Ken. One step at a time."

So the race was reduced to a simple formula: put one foot in front of the other; then give the other foot a turn. I stared only at my dusty boots, praying they would not become smoking boots. I certainly didn't want to end up some crispy critter smoldering on the mountainside. We inched upward until finally a cool blast of air announced our arrival at the top of the ridge. We didn't stop to celebrate but yelled like idiots as we hurried down the other side of the mountain. We had beaten the storm. We were alive!

We succeeded by going one step at a time. I did it with the encouragement of a faithful friend who knew I had it in me, even when I wasn't so sure. Danny remains one of those treasured men in my life who remind me that living fully alive is only as complicated as the next step I take. At sixty-five, I weigh 185 pounds and have a resting heart rate under fifty and the blood pressure of a twenty-five-year-old. I no longer fight debilitating depression, and my family says I'm much more fun to live with. Step by step, telephone pole by telephone pole—physically, mentally, and spiritually—I'm pressing toward the purpose for which I was created.

So what is your ultimate goal? What is the first step you need to take, and what are the telephone poles that will keep you moving toward the mark?

Chapter Nine

ONE IS
A LONELY NUMBER

I WAS SPEAKING TO A GATHERING OF PASTORS FROM AROUND the world at a conference designed to help churches develop small-group ministries. I addressed the importance of churches having a place where people could develop deep friendships. As I delivered the talk, my own heart began to ache. Even as I spoke, my soul yearned for significant, intimate relationships. I had to fight to keep my emotions from boiling to the surface.

My insane travel schedule was definitely an obstacle to establishing solid friendships, but I couldn't use it as an excuse any more than I could use it for an excuse not to exercise. For years I'd been unwilling to do the work required to make close friends, and I was unwilling to pay the price. As a result, I was surrounded by fans but woefully short of friends. That day I confessed to my audience a fear I had shared with my wife, Diane.

I had a recurring dream that I had died. In my dream Diane managed to handle her grief fairly well, but she couldn't find six friends close enough to take a day off and carry the box I was to be buried in. In my out-of-body dream, I watched helplessly as she pulled the casket down the cold cement steps alone . . . *thump, thump, thump* . . . then dragged it to where the big black SUV waited.

My situation is not unique. I have met hundreds of people who felt they had no friends at all. The surprising discovery was that many of them did not know how to make friends or, like me, were afraid to try.

YOU NEED A FRIEND

You might be able to survive without friends, but you cannot live fully alive. In our culture it's possible to be surrounded by work colleagues, neighbors, teammates, classmates, and even fans, without having someone who makes that deeply satisfying, heart-to-heart connection that defines real friendship. As I finished my talk that day, I knew I needed to be more intentional about finding friends who would do life with me. I realized I couldn't live fully alive alone.

So how did I find friends in a desert of acquaintances? I did it the same way I raced the thunderstorm to the top of a mountain ridge: one step at a time. My first step was to assess what was required to develop close friendships and purposefully change my lifestyle to make it happen.

Bill Gothard, founder of the Institute in Basic Life Principles, categorizes friendships on four levels:

1. An *acquaintance* is a person you contact rarely or only once, such as someone you meet while traveling or who comes to your house to fix the plumbing or washing machine. I had tens of thousands of these.

2. A *casual friendship* is based on common interests or activities. A casual friend may be a person at work or someone you know at a club, at church, or on a sports team. I had dozens of these kinds of friends.

3. A *close friendship* is based on mutual life goals and long-term interests. The two of you see potential achievement in each other's lives. You discuss specific goals and assume a personal responsibility for developing them. These friends can make suggestions about important aspects of your life. I had very few of these. Not enough to carry a box.

4. An *intimate friendship* is based on open honesty, discretion, and a commitment to the development of each other's character and spiritual potential. You help each other through trials and sorrows. You assume personal responsibility for each other's reputation. You are sensitive to traits and attitudes that you both need to improve. Intimate friends are committed to faithfulness, loyalty, and availability.[1] Other than Diane, I couldn't think of a single intimate friendship I had developed or maintained in the past five years of my life.

Life is at its best when we are developing friends in all of these categories. People seeking intimate friendship don't knock at your door and volunteer for the job. If someone does, you should probably run. The scariest people in the world are those who appear to be desperate in their search for friends. There's a sense of panic and a loud sucking sound that emanates from these souls. You don't want to sound like a vacuum cleaner. Take a deep breath. Relax.

I found it effective to mine my existing acquaintances for people who might become casual friends. I spent some time with casual friends and was delighted to watch some of those relationships grow into close friendships. Eventually the effort paid off, and over time I found relationships that touched my soul. It didn't happen overnight. I had to work at it, make the investment, take the risk, and extend lots of grace. It's possible for an intimate friendship to develop from any of the other categories of friendship, and it's worth the work. Today I have enough friends to carry the box, and if Diane hires a couple more, they will be able to carry it down the steps without dropping it.

One of the culprits keeping me from close friendships was that old nemesis, fear. I'd had a few friendships end painfully, usually because I was unwilling to allow anyone to confront me. I was also fearful of confronting my friends. When the going got tough, I bolted. What a conundrum! True friendship *is* painful. It requires the courage to walk through fire as well as dance in the rain. I wanted to dance, but I was afraid of the heat.

When I look back at crashing in that shallow bathtub at the edge of the road, digging snow out of my underwear with a stabbing pain in my wrist, I vividly remember begging God that I might have some of this joy and adventure in all of my life. Yet when it came to the commitment necessary to develop deep friendships, I was afraid to point the sled downhill and let go. What if I broke my wrist? What if a UPS truck pulled out in front of the relationship? What if it hurt? A spirit of boldness, screaming down an icy road in a plastic saucer, was missing when it came to matters of the heart. I was a coward, unwilling to face the possibility of rejection and unwilling to carve out the time to build significant relationships.

Without risk, friendship will never be anything but a distant dream.

For a while I leaned heavily on the rush that comes from applause and laughter to sustain me. How crazy is that? Fans see you as networking potential; friends see your potential. Fans love you for your performance; friends love you for you. Fans are fickle; friends stick with you through the toughest times. Fans want to see only your good side; friends protect your backside. Fans demand that you entertain them; friends are satisfied just to be with you. I cherish and appreciate my fans, but friends interact with me and nurture me on a deeper level than fans are able to do.

Making friends is like exercise; it requires discipline and vigilance. I stopped trying to pretend I was perfect and stopped requiring perfection from the people around me. I found some of my best friends by looking for ways to befriend people. I made investments in the lives of people who were already in my life.

IT'S ABOUT TIME

In the end it all boiled down to time—time sharing meals, time helping move furniture, time sitting by a hospital bed. Not very dramatic and mysterious, is it? Making friends is laughing until the early hours of morning or talking on a back porch until you fall asleep. It's celebrating a birthday. Sometimes it's just being there in a time of crisis and saying nothing.

I had to learn to trust someone with the real me. On stage I feel safe because I'm in control. Face-to-face, I'm vulnerable. It's hard to reveal my heart, my weaknesses, my dreams, and just as hard to listen to the heartaches and dreams of others. I took a risk by making myself accountable to someone else. I was a terrible accountability partner to myself. It was too easy to lie to myself, then believe the lie. I started learning to risk by holding my friends accountable. We would push each other to stay on track in every area of life. We refused to let each other give up on dreams. We challenged each other's views. We argued, intervened, cheered, and encouraged.

The greatest risk in the search for true friendship is rejection. Along the way I was dumped by a valued friend of many years. I still love my friend, but I miss that intimate interaction that once characterized our relationship. I miss the laughter, the soul searching, the energizing arguments, and the friendly games of poker.

Losing a friend is an excruciating experience. The temptation is strong never to take that kind of risk again, never to let anyone that close to my heart. Then I remember the sled ride again. Pain was part of the price I had to pay for the joy of the ride, proof that I was alive. Waterskiing and friendship have something in common. If you choose to risk your heart with friends, you will fall; it will hurt, but it will be worth it.

Part of the wonderful new life I have discovered is a circle of great friends and a handful of remarkable, intimate, personal friends. I can exist without intimate personal friends. I did it for years. But I can't live fully alive without intimate friends, and neither can you.

FAITHFUL FRIENDS

Friends were critical to the physical challenges in my life. Since my shocking encounter with The "Noooooo!" Photo, the process of getting fit has been painful and discouraging at times, and at times exhilarating. Part of the way, I've had friends to share my journey toward better fitness. Other times, I've tried it alone. Take it from me: you can't do it alone. Living fully alive is not a solo act. Trying to make it alone is a recipe for failure.

Human beings are social creatures. We were created to interact with others, love each other, and depend on each other.

If I expect to maintain this new lifestyle and continue to enjoy its benefits, I must find friends and like-minded people who will join me in the quest; people who will help hold my feet to the fire; friends who will spur me on when I feel discouraged and who will celebrate my achievements with me.

As much as I enjoy a solitary ride through the countryside on my bicycle, I need the company and encouragement of faithful friends to keep me honest. It's almost impossible to stay in bed if someone is knocking at your door to run with you. Some of my friends and I actually ended up forming our own club, which we christened GAG for Guts and Glory. We wanted to get rid of our guts, and we wanted to glorify God by taking good care of our bodies. We also studied the Bible and wanted to have the strength, mental toughness, and endurance to experience everything God wanted for us.

Several of us who signed up to run the triathlon trained together, riding bicycles and running up and down the Tennessee hills. One morning we tackled the steep and infamous Yardstick Hill near my house. As I pedaled, puffed, and grunted toward the top, I looked back to see Jacob, a fellow GAG member, struggling to make headway. This was his first attempt at Yardstick Hill, but he kept plugging along, going slower and slower yet refusing to get off the bike. Halfway up he began traversing back and forth across the road. I could hear him gasping for air as sweat poured from his body. When he finally got to the top he jumped from his bike and raised his arms in victory. We hollered like a couple of high school cheerleaders.

Later in that ride we started up another hill, two miles long. Halfway up, I had my friends stop so I could take some pictures of them. We paused on the steep, hot ribbon of asphalt. Behind us the beautiful Natchez Trace Parkway Bridge majestically spanned the road we were riding. Only a few moments earlier we had crossed underneath that bridge. Ahead, the road snaked relentlessly up and through the trees before disappearing over the crest.

As I snapped the last picture and we prepared to continue the climb, my friend Theron stayed put, his feet firmly planted on the pavement on either side of his bike. "I've used all I've got," he said. "I don't have any strength left. I can't make it to the top."

"Yes, you can," I barked. "You have more strength than you think you have." My challenge drew a confused stare. "Imagine that your daughter was at the top of this hill and only you could save her life, and the only way you could do it was to get on that bicycle and ride up there as quickly as you could. If she were there and needed you, would you have anything left?"

He nodded vigorously, still trying to catch his breath.

"Well, she's up there," I said. "Go get her."

He was gone before I finished the sentence and rode at a substantial pace the rest of the way up the hill.

What we really mean when we say we don't have anything left is, "I'm extremely uncomfortable. I'm breathing hard. My legs hurt." In reality there's plenty left if you have the right motivation—or the purposeful encouragement of a friend.

On several occasions I've been the one who couldn't go on. I remember during a battle with debilitating depression, a true friend sat by my side and encouraged me. "God has abandoned me," I said.

"No, He hasn't," she insisted.

My sister had flown hundreds of miles to be with me during this difficult time. "You've been blinded to signs of His presence all around you," she told me. "Look!" She pointed to the sun streaming through a skylight, bathing my body in its warmth. "Open your eyes!"

I recalled a scripture I had learned as a child. As I remembered it, Psalm 121 begins: "I will lift up mine eyes unto the hills, from whence cometh my help" (KJV). That was a significant moment in restoring my sight and my sanity. My sister did for me what I had done for Theron. It's what friends do for each other.

You might be the one stuck and out of juice on the side of the road. You might be the one down in the dumps and ready to shift your life into neutral, or you could be the one who inspires the weary to keep on going.

God says where two or more are gathered together, He comes to the meeting (Matt. 18:20). And if He's there, the resources for creativity, spiritual growth, and physical endurance are also there in infinite abundance. We need each other. Start your physical program for health alone if you must, but quickly find like-minded friends to do it with you. Keelan Hastings is a trainer who pushes me way beyond where I would go alone. He is also my friend, so I know he cares. If you need spiritual growth, find some friends who want to take that ride with you. Find a friend who will help you track your progress and urge you on when you fall behind. Find a trusted mentor, teacher, or pastor who will be a friend and spur you on toward the top of the mountain.

MIKE

A few years ago I met Mike Lahouti, a man who would become one of my best friends. He taught me another truth about living fully alive: we should not limit our friends to people of like mind. He and I were opposite poles of a magnet. He was a successful, organized sales rep for an international corporation, and I was a scatterbrained entertainer. I was training to run tri-athlons, and he had little interest in physical activity. He was raised as a Muslim, and I was raised in a devout Christian home. Mike was not fond of what he knew of Christianity, but he was intensely curious about the faith he saw demonstrated in the home of Brian and Traci, my son-in-law and daughter, and was head-over-heels in love with my grandchildren. His love for my family was the one thing we had in common.

Mike lived next door to Traci and Brian and would often drop in unannounced for dinner. He expected us to reciprocate. His home was always filled with friends and laughter and food. At the sound of his back door opening, we would hear the excited shout, "Welcome! Come in. Sit down. Eat." It didn't take long for Mike to become an adored and trusted friend.

Once I got to know Mike, I discovered that we shared other common ground. He was stubborn and opinionated, and so am I. He was open to hearing the views of others, and so am I. He also had a marvelous sense of humor and a laugh that could melt Arctic ice. Almost every night Mike and my son-in-law would sit on the back porch, talking about the things that only true friends can discuss and still remain friends—faith, politics, personal strengths and weaknesses, family struggles.

At Christmas I gave Mike a Bible inscribed with his name, and he began to read it. Eventually we started an unconventional Bible study that will remain one of my most cherished memories: stale sandwiches and wine followed by an informal clutch of people sprawled across furniture or on the floor with open Bibles. Mike and my family and a few neighbors studied the book of Romans, then the book of Acts. Mike's questions were intelligent, probing, and firm. For some of them, we had no answers. We made no secret of our desire to see Mike come to know Christ and the power of His resurrection.

In the summer of 2010, Mike began to lose his long and courageous battle with cancer. We often dropped in to check on his health and nurture this valued friendship. My little grandchildren drew encouraging pictures and wrote notes declaring their unabashed love. Once they brought Mike a crayon drawing of him standing in heaven on clouds with Jesus. We never did figure out which one was Jesus. Evidently Jesus and Mike resemble one another. My initial fears about the pictures causing Mike anxiety were unfounded. He took great comfort in the love expressed by these children and was deeply moved by their desire to see him experience faith in Christ.

As Mike's health went into steep decline, Brian took him to a clinic to see if they could prescribe some relief for his pain. There in the waiting room of the clinic, curiosity, love, and friendship arrived simultaneously at the intersection of faith. Mike surrendered to the love of Christ and sparked a moving celebration in our circle of friends. Cancer is a cruel disease, and the end of Mike's life was not exempt from pain or sorrow. But the comfort of God's love and the assurance of eternal life gave Mike, his family, and those who loved him a memory of hope that we will treasure forever. Mike stepped from life as we know it to life as it was meant to be: cancer-free, pain-free, sorrow-free, fully alive in the presence of the One who made him and loved him most. Where did it start? With a disarming, dangerous, risky, wonderful, painful thing called friendship.

THE CONSUMMATION
OF FRIENDSHIP

As I was writing these words, my phone buzzed. I glanced down at a text that froze my heart. Another friend, David Pierce, was in the hospital. His kidneys had suddenly failed, and he was seriously ill. I quickly sent out a message on Twitter and Facebook, requesting prayers for my friend. Then I called Mike Smith, one of my GAG buddies, and told him of the situation. Immediately Mike said, "I need to go down to the hospital and see David. Do you want to go along?"

My immediate response was to delay any trip to the hospital until I finished the work I was doing on this book. When my computer screen flashed to life, my face flushed with shame. How can I write a chapter on the cost of friendship and not put everything aside to visit my friend whose life might be in danger? In David's book *To Kill a Zombie*, he had written a hilarious and touching chapter on the value of our friendship. I had come close to exchanging that value for a few hours of work. I called Mike and told him, of course, I would go with him to see David. We had a wonderful visit. An hour of laughter and love and prayer restored color to David's face and lifted all of our spirits. No text or tweet could replace what happened in that room. The doctors found the source of David's problem, and today he's home and living fully alive.

And speaking of Twitter, what about those cyberfriendships? Are social-network "friends" really friends? The Internet today allows us to delve into deeply personal subjects with people we've never met and scarcely know. How do these relationships fit into the categories of friendship, if at all? I'm not sure myself. But I wonder, how close can friends be when they're physically isolated? Loneliness ages us faster and more drastically than anything else in life. By that I don't mean a feeling of loneliness; I mean being alone to the point where we stop physically interacting with old friends and no longer make new ones.

One of the ironies of modern life is that the more technically interconnected we get, the more isolated and disconnected we seem to be. A friend recently told me about going to dinner at a restaurant and seeing a party of young adults come in to celebrate a birthday. They were all dressed in festive clothes and the birthday girl had a bunch of balloons tied to her chair. But after everyone was seated, one by one they fished out their iPhones. Within minutes, all eight of them sat silently around the table, oblivious to each other and the occasion, staring into their tiny screens, lost in their individual cyberworlds. There was a birthday party going on, but no one was there to enjoy it.

I won't dispute that there is great value to the social networks and cyberfriends we enjoy. Even God used His own unique brand of social media. When He wanted to reveal the Ten Commandments, He introduced the first "iRock." I imagine that Moses' friends were quite offended when he kept glancing at it at the dinner table. Like most devices, it broke.

When God wanted to warn King Belshazzar of impending disaster, He released the first stunning version of the iPad: a mysterious finger wrote the ominous message of imminent destruction on a screen the size of a wall.

When God wanted to give the Israelites directions to the promised land, He released the first GPS, with a guidance system that worked day and night, and even had a recalculating feature.

But when God wanted to demonstrate His love for us, it required nothing less than flesh meeting flesh. Though in times past He had communicated using all kinds of wonderful gadgets, in order to communicate His love, He sent Jesus to meet people face-to-face. The tablets and burning bushes were replaced with dinners, embraces, personal touch, and holy blood spilled on barren ground.

I'm so glad God didn't text, e-mail, or tweet His message of love to us. Only the appearance of God in the flesh could consummate the relationship He desired with us. It was this act of love that gave us the ability to lighten up and live fully alive.

Honestly, I don't want to downplay the value of social media. It's often a wonderful entrée to live friendships that last for years. But if we confuse communication with communion, we miss friendship.

What rescues us from this trend toward isolation? True friends who pull us away from the computer, iPod, television, or whatever is connected to those things stuck in our ears, and bring us back to the rich, real world of conversation with flesh-and-blood human beings.

Keep refreshing your supply of friends in all categories. We live in a society that is terrified of strangers. What's the worst that can happen if you offer to sit with someone who is eating alone? He might say he wants to be left alone. So be it. He might think you're weird. Big deal! He'd be right! It's a risk worth taking. That new acquaintance might just become the friend you need. Reaching out to people is supposed to be one of the marks of a Christian. It's certainly the mark of someone who is living fully alive.

Even if I could succeed by myself, I have no desire to stand on the pinnacle of a mountain celebrating my achievements alone. Besides, I don't think I'd ever get there solo. One is a lonely number.

Jesus had twelve guys on His team. I'm not Jesus, so I'll settle for two or three! Seek out people to do life with you. In the end, you're going to need at least six.

Chapter Ten

FINDING YOUR SWEET SPOT

I REMEMBER PICKING UP A HITCHHIKER IN THE MID '60S ON the icy country roads of northern Minnesota. His name was Lance. After warming up in the car, Lance told me how he had left a stable environment and a good job to wander the country, doing odd jobs and occasionally begging for money to get by. When I asked why he was doing this, he replied, "I'm trying to find myself."

Trying to be funny I said, "Good news, Lance! I found you! It has been reported you are sitting in my car."

"No," he said. "I don't need *you* to find me; I need *me* to find me."

I sniffed for evidence of alcohol, but Lance was sober and serious. "So you're lost?" I asked. "I never thought of it that way," he said, and then was quiet for a long time. Little did I know that forty-five years from that moment a little girl would say to her rescuers, "My grandpa is lost!" and I would begin my own search for the person God had made me to be.

Finding yourself is much harder if you have no idea of your spiritual lineage or purpose in life. We are uniquely created in the image of God. We are wired to find the most joy in life by living out that uniqueness. My rider was not alone in his quest. People spend enormous amounts of energy and money trying to find themselves, often searching for that sweet spot of living fully alive in places it can't be found. You don't have to circle the globe, bungee jump from a cliff, or retreat into a cave to find yourself. Those activities will certainly stir your soul as surely as a wild sled ride down a mountain road, but they're not a requirement for living fully alive. The quest is not as difficult as it might seem. It might require a mirror.

Remember the essence of the Saint Irenaeus quote? The glory of God is man fully alive. That means more than simply being off life-support or the critical list. It means more than reaching the pinnacle of income, productivity, or recognition. It goes deeper than just being fit and physically healthy. When we are fully alive we function at the capacity we were created for in every area of life. We operate on all cylinders—mentally, physically, socially, and spiritually—doing what most glorifies God and brings Him joy. God's sweet spot and our sweet spot share the same address.

So how are you wired? If you don't know, how do you find out? Take some time to think through your life. What makes you feel complete, satisfied, and convinced that you're doing what God put you here to do? If you could invest your life in something and money was no object, what would you do? What do you do now that touches the lives of others and brings them joy? What do other people say you do well? Write down some of your answers. I know what some of my answers would be. I leave a fabulous party with a warm glow of comfort and a full stomach, but the pleasure I feel in that moment doesn't compare to what I feel when I watch people laugh until they hurt and have the privilege to bring them hope and faith in the process. What in your life has given you a purpose bigger than just satisfying the most recent desire sticking its head above the surface?

Maybe the secret is what I heard Charles "Tremendous" Jones say years ago at a Promise Keepers rally: "There are two kinds of people in the world, takers and givers. The takers eat better. The givers sleep better."

Rick Warren touched a chord with his runaway best seller, *The Purpose Driven Life*. I remember the surge of resistance I felt when I read this statement early in his book: "It's not about you!"[1] But he was right. It really is about glorifying God with our lives. It's not about what you can *get* but what you can *give*. You will never glimpse life at its best until you draw from an inspiration bigger than yourself. Happiness and fulfillment come from glorifying Him even when there's sacrifice involved. That is the sweet spot. We were created to find the greatest joy and fulfillment by serving God and others with whatever gift God has given us.

We've heard a million times that material things don't deliver the fulfillment God intended for us. For many years I proclaimed that truth without really experiencing it. Then I reached a point in life when I had most of the things I wanted: a nice home, an airplane, a successful career—and an emptiness that shouldn't have been there. Perhaps I had missed the boat to paradise. Maybe what I was missing could be found somewhere else.

As a young adult my exploration for living fully alive led me to some barren and dangerous territory. I knew the truth but was unwilling to commit to it. I discovered from painful experience that what glitters so enticingly as the answer to the quest for abundant life often dims once grasped. The desires to gain and keep possessions, fame and recognition, and excursions from purity and integrity quickly claim our time and energy yet fail to deliver on quenching the greatest thirst of all. Even worse, these excursions often lead to death rather than life.

Years ago I heard a story of how primitive people would catch monkeys, which for them were a source of food. They would drill a small hole in a coconut and pour out the milk. Then they would tie the coconut to a tree and place a morsel of food inside to attract the monkeys. Inevitably a monkey would come, reach through the hole, and grab whatever was inside. Once its fist was wrapped around the morsel, the monkey was unable to pull its hand out of the hole. Only by letting go could its hand slip free. When the hunters came, they would kill the monkey with clubs. Even when threatened with death the monkey would not let go, and in death it could not hang on to what it had so foolishly cherished. Momentary material things can be wonderful blessings, but they cannot sustain life and are not the source of living fully alive.

If he or she is honest, any celebrity or enormously successful person will confirm this truth. In an interview with Ted Turner, Barbara Walters asked what it was like to have such power, wealth, and fame. Ted answered, "It's an empty bag."[2] How sad that so many of us refuse to believe that truth because we've never touched the bag. We won't take someone else's word for it. We're willing to expend our lives and our talents to peek inside, just to see for ourselves if the sweet spot is there.

I heard someone say that the charity work of celebrities is not just a publicity stunt—it is a genuine search for meaning. And many of them find it is the most meaningful thing they do. When Piers Morgan asked George Clooney whether he gets angry when people say he's wasting his time in Sudan and that his charity work is for "self-aggrandizing reasons," Clooney answered, "I don't need to be more famous. I've got all the attention I need, and I'm just trying to use that attention for other people."[3]

MINE YOUR LIFE FOR MEMORIES

So how do you find yourself? How do you discover the way you're wired and what God designed you to be? Memories often contain your first hints. If you trace your life back through the doors of past experiences, those doors open to reveal earlier passageways leading to rooms with still other doors slightly ajar. Those doors then lead to more rooms and older memories. Many wondrous and magical moments are uncovered until finally you arrive at the last door.

When that door creaked open for me, I was standing beside a large radio. This thing was the size of a desk with huge volume- and station-selection dials that moved needles across a brightly lit display of radio frequency numbers. On top was a lid that, when opened, revealed the magical apparatus of an old LP record player. I can close my eyes and see it today. There I stood, all chubby, diaper hanging low, listening to a now ancient comedy radio show. When the audience laughed and applauded, I would scream with delight. I loved it. My screaming got me in big trouble that day. Perhaps that's why the memory is so vivid. I don't think it's a coincidence that I've worked to hear that laughter all my life, and I've been in trouble ever since.

I think the memory is also vivid because on that day God drove a small stake into the ground—a tiny marker, the first of many, to help me understand what I was designed to do.

I found another clue in high school. My teenage years were a difficult period of my life. I weighed 110–115 pounds and got bullied a lot in school. I was a slow bloomer without a stitch of athletic ability. I had the eye-hand coordination of a carp and was further hampered by a congenital curvature of the bone in both my arms. Throwing and catching balls were an integral part of being a teenage boy, and I could do neither well. But I have a stubborn streak that makes it hard for me to give up. How fascinating that God gave me a fiercely competitive spirit and nothing to back it up.

As I wandered through the musty caves of my memory, I discovered, almost hidden in the rocks, another stake God had placed in my life, a marker that contained hints of what I was designed to be. It all began when a visiting physical education instructor decided to administer an eye-hand coordination test. The entire test revolved around catching a football while running full speed ahead. When my turn came, I couldn't catch it. I couldn't even catch it standing still. Over and over the ball slipped from my fingers and tumbled across the ground. Finally in frustration the teacher gave up.

In front of my classmates he said, "Go take a shower. You will never amount to anything."

"You will never amount to anything!" Those words echoed in my soul for years. In retrospect, I suppose he thought I wasn't trying hard enough. Perhaps he wanted to motivate me to toughen up, become a man. Evidently, for him, becoming a man was synonymous with catching a football. At the time I didn't fully grasp it—pardon the pun—but I wasn't created to catch footballs. I wasn't designed to be an athlete. I was designed to be weird—to see the world through a different lens than most people do.

From the day I stood beside the giant radio until today, I have found great delight in making people laugh. When I was a teenager I used my gift of weird as a defense mechanism to keep from being beaten up. If I could make people laugh, they wouldn't hit me. Later it became a way for me to get attention. I wanted people to value me. When people were laughing, it was the closest I felt to being loved and, strangely enough, the closest I felt to God. I wanted that applause I heard on the radio.

As misguided as my motivation might have been in the beginning, it was my first taste of being fully alive and the first clue to how I was wired. Each time I could make people laugh I could forget for a moment those hurtful words—"You will never amount to anything!" Then one day something happened that set me on a path I would follow to this day.

I loved English. I loved literature. I never mentioned these passions to my schoolmates because I would risk another beating for being a sissy. My English teacher was Frances W. Peterson, and I remember we were studying *Macbeth*. When we came to that infamous line, "Out, out damned spot," I raised my hand and suggested several other very inappropriate adjectives that could be substituted for the word *damned*. My classmates exploded in laughter, but I saw the look of disappointment on Mrs. Peterson's face. She made me stay after school. Back in those days, when you stayed after school, it meant you missed your bus and the teacher called your parents to come get you. And when they came, they didn't bring a lawyer; they brought instruments of discipline: belts, switches, and occasionally a two-by-four. I was in trouble.

Mrs. Peterson pulled my desk right up to hers, and as I waited for my parents to arrive, she sat silently grading papers. Finally she pushed her work aside and fixed her eyes on me. I can still see her long, slender fingers as she capped her pen, folded her hands, and said, "Kenneth Alpheus Davis, look at me." I had been rude and profane. None of that was tolerated in my school. I knew I was going to be expelled. I looked at her. Her face was a mosaic of anger and sadness.

I expected her to spit out a proclamation of my expulsion. At minimum I was braced for a stern lecture. I winced when she spoke. "God has given you a gift," she said, somewhat sadly. She turned and looked out the window for a moment. This is not what I had expected. I had thrown nothing but dirt at her, and she had chosen to push it all aside to find a nugget of gold, which she was now holding in front of me. She looked back and continued. "You've been using this gift to destroy my class. That's going to stop. I want you to go out for speech."

"I can't try out for speech!" This was a humiliating prospect. All of my friends walked the halls with letter jackets that had macho symbols sewn into the fabric—hockey sticks, footballs, track shoes with wings. I wasn't about to walk around with a set of lips stitched on my chest. I might as well wear a sign that said "Kick me."

Her response was immediate. "You will go out for speech because the alternative is unthinkable." Mrs. Peterson had caught a glimpse of what I'd felt standing in front of the radio years before, and now she was intent on helping me develop what she called "a gift from God." "You will enter our speech program in the category of humorous interpretation." Judgment had been passed. Justice had been done. When I close my eyes, I can almost see her pounding a gavel and proclaiming, "Case closed. You have value, and I will prove it." It was incredible. I got to tell jokes and make my weird observations—the weirder and funnier, the better. I would be rewarded for it with the sweet sound of laughter and applause. In the coming years I would be showered with that reward.

I felt something in my temple that day: a warm, pleasant throbbing. It was a pulse. It was my heart beating, telling me, "God did not make a mistake when He made you. He gave you a unique gift. Now, for His sake, use it. You are alive. Start to live!"

Years later I got a chance to publicly thank Mrs. Peterson for the influence she had in my life. Her words, "God has given you a gift," wiped away the horrible words, "You will never amount to anything!" They moved me from fear to confidence. They helped me realize that I didn't have to be like everyone else. I didn't have to win at everything I tried. It was okay to be me because God had made me. This wonderful teacher put me on a path to living fully alive. I didn't know until years later that with that same gavel I had imagined, Mrs. Peterson had driven a stake in the ground that would help me look back and see a divine trend taking place in my life.

LIVE WHAT YOU BELIEVE

Along the way there were others who confirmed I was on the right path and insisted that I move with purpose and excellence. I went on to college knowing I could succeed in speech, but I wasn't pursuing excellence in other areas. I put all my effort into what I could do well and blew off everything else. One day my philosophy professor, Robert Thompson, a friend and someone I respected, called me into his office and asked me what I wanted out of life. I said, "I want to live out every bit of potential God created within me. I want it all."

Mr. Thompson pushed up his wire-rimmed glasses and leaned back in his chair. He never took his eyes from mine. The room was awkwardly silent when he spoke.

"You're lying," he said.

"Excuse me?" I squeaked.

This was serious business, especially since it was coming from one of my favorite professors. He shoved my last test paper across the table. I stared at the failing grade scrawled in red across the top. "You have the capacity to ace every test I give you. You are intelligent and can think critically. It's a gift! But you will never reach your potential until you're willing to put forth the effort. Your actions need to match your words. I'll believe what you say when you live what you say you believe. If you want to be everything God created you to be, there's where you can start."

He waited until I looked up. He was not smiling, and he took time to adjust his glasses again. "Never fail another test I give you."

As I left the room, he called my name. I turned. "Now show me what you've got!" he said. This time he was smiling.

From that moment on I passed every test he gave me. Not because he scared me into action but because I recognized that what he said was absolutely true. Wow, I was funny, and smart, and lazy! I knew there was something I could do to change at least one of those things. This was a lesson I never forgot. I couldn't squander what God had given me. The gifts He had designed into my life shaped me and became part of my quest to live fully alive.

What moments in your life are guiding you now? What long-held goals and dreams are you still trying to fulfill?

Later in life I would take a test developed by Dick Hagstrom, a man who had invested in my life by sharing his wisdom and friendship. The test enabled Dick to identify the one essential element a person needed in order to be fulfilled and happy in life. It identified a person's unique design and what satisfied and inspired him or her most. One person might be wired to be creative, where another needed to work with his hands. Some people, like inventors, needed to make new discoveries, and others were most satisfied when they could nurture and enable others.

That essence might not be found in the person's job, but Dick believed that if an individual wanted to be fulfilled in life, he had to find a way to express it. He might do it through a hobby or as a volunteer or during time off work. The key was for that person to discover what God had placed within him that inspired him at the most fundamental level to feel fully alive and then find a way to do it.

I took Dick's test and walked into his office to get the results. Sitting behind a neatly organized oak desk, he was a big man with jet-black hair. Without a word he stood to his feet and started clapping his hands together.

My inspiration was applause?

He explained that it wasn't the applause itself. That was only an outward sign of what really satisfied me most: recognition. "You could not ghostwrite a book," he said. "You could not sit anonymously in a research lab and develop medicine to save the lives of thousands of people who would never know your name. You must see the results of your labor, and the sooner the better."

I sank into the nearest couch like a deflated balloon. "I'm a narcissist."

"No," Dick said, "this is the way God has wired you. What you need to do is find a way to reflect that applause back to Him. It's a gift He gave you to glorify Him." Suddenly I was whisked back in time and was standing beside that huge radio, screaming in delight at the sound of laughter and applause. I heard Mrs. Peterson's voice: "God has given you a gift." I heard Mr. Thompson's tough but honest challenge to practice what I spoke. On the way back to the present, I glanced at the stakes and the direction they were leading me. I had walked the path of making people laugh to avoid a black eye. I had sought applause for evidence of my worth. I had reached for recognition and fame. All of these experiences had brought me closer to the desire of my life now. I want to glorify God with everything that I am. I want to know Christ and the power of His resurrection. I want to live fully alive.

God doesn't make mistakes. But He does plant stakes to help us see our design.

Not everybody is the same. Joy Groblebe doesn't care about applause. She doesn't need to get credit for her work. She wants only the freedom to do what she does best. Joy loves providing the support and marketing to help other people realize their dreams. "I do what frees up my clients to do what only they can do," she explains. "I help them live fully alive and that makes me feel fully alive."

The first time Joy expressed this desire, her sister responded, "Why would you want to be someone's secretary?" But Joy's creativity, enthusiasm, and unique gift of seeing what needs to be done make her much more than a secretary. She puts feet to dreams. In the words of Seth Godin, Joy is a linchpin, an irreplaceable part of any team she is on.

Joy lit up when she was offered the job as executive assistant to the general manager of KMOX, the largest radio station in St. Louis. Her boss gave her every project she could handle and the complete freedom to call the shots to make it happen—even the freedom to make mistakes. Good boss! Joy relished the challenge. "I felt like I had the best job of anyone in the company," she said. "I got to identify problems and opportunities and take care of business." No spotlight, no applause, no big title, just the satisfaction of a job well done.

Lucky for me Joy is now my executive assistant. I don't know what I would do without her. Joy was invaluable in helping us bring the movie *Fully Alive* to theaters around the country and was the catalyst for developing the Fully Alive curriculum. Without her help this book never would have been written. On top of all this she runs a successful business from her garage, making and marketing cupcake tower stands.

And here's the kicker: Joy also has four small children. She knows that being a mom and having the creative freedom to enable people such as myself are the two things that inspire her most, so she and her husband have figured out a way she can work from home. This morning while talking with Joy on the phone, I heard a tiny voice ask for marshmallows. Sound unprofessional? Considering that most people would kill to have someone like Joy taking care of business, freeing them to do what they do best, I'm happy to hear a little voice asking for marshmallows. From early in her life Joy could identify what "turned her crank," as my father used to say. She doesn't need credit. Her reward is seeing others succeed.

Sometimes I'm tempted to think, *I want to be like Joy!*

I couldn't if I tried. Looking back on my life, I can see the unmistakable succession of markers that are an essential part of my operations manual. We're all wired in a divinely unique way. Find a way to live out your uniqueness to the glory of God.

A WORD OF CAUTION

It's easy to get offtrack here. Although there's nothing wrong with competition or achievement, living fully alive isn't necessarily about either. As I took time to look back and discover stakes God had driven in my life, I found another one at my alma mater, Oak Hills College. After my experience in high school, I knew I would breeze through speech class in college. Phil Van Wynen was the professor, and I could hardly wait to impress him with my talent as a speaker. The assignment for the very first day of class was for every student to give a speech. As I listened to each of my classmates, my confidence and conceit grew. *It was so sad that they didn't have the experience and training I had enjoyed.* Then it was my turn. In the short time allowed, I gave them the best of my humor and persuasion and concluded with an unforgettable illustration. The response from the class was wonderful, and even Professor Van Wynen seemed impressed. I had given the best speech of anyone in my class.

You can imagine my surprise when I received the average grade of C for my stellar presentation. I marched indignantly into the professor's office. He listened patiently as I told him of my experience and achievements as a speaker, pointed out weaknesses in the speeches of my classmates, and demanded to know why I had received a grade of C. "In this class you are not competing against anyone," he said. "And you will not be graded on your *ability*. You will be graded on your *teachability* and your ability to improve." Every person who gave a speech that day had received a C. Future grades would be based on that benchmark. Although I walked from the building that day with wounded pride dragging from my spirit like toilet paper on a wet shoe, I fell in love with that class. And with that professor. Growth is far more exciting and challenging than competition. Phil Van Wynen was an educator par excellence. He knew that unique giftedness is not to be displayed like a trophy; it is to be honed and developed to bring glory to God. Every person who attended his class left the class a winner.

Find your sweet spot, and as the army challenges its recruits, "Be all you can be!" Or as my friend McNair Wilson so brilliantly challenges his audience, "If you don't do *you*, you doesn't get done, and the world is incomplete."

Chapter Eleven

LIGHTEN UP!

I LOVE THE WORD *LIGHT* WITH ALL ITS VARIANT AND SUBTLE inflections. It describes the agent that stimulates sight and makes things visible, like that which emanates from a light bulb. The light in someone's eyes is a wonderful indication that the person is alive. Light in someone's eyes can also indicate understanding of truth or mystery: "She saw the light." It can indicate mischievousness or ardent love. The word can also be used to describe that which produces flame. It indicates that something is not burdensome or heavy. It creates the idea of energy and motivation: "Someone light a fire under that guy!" We have skylights, traffic lights, northern lights; Jesus said, "I am the light of the world" (John 8:12). Almost every variation of the word has a positive connotation to it. Darkness and light are mutually exclusive. In every sense of the word *light*, this chapter will encourage you to "lighten up"—and live.

Life is a long journey, and those who want to get the most out of it must travel light, unburdened of anything that would destroy the joy of the journey or keep them from reaching their destination. That's one of the reasons I admire the apostle Paul so much. He was single-minded in his purpose and shed everything that couldn't help him achieve that purpose. Often when I find myself bogged down I remember his words: "I want to know Christ and the power of his resurrection" (Phil. 3:10).

He was also honest. This once legalistic, hypocritical Pharisee confessed that he hadn't yet reached his goal and didn't have it all together, but he wasn't about to quit.

In regard to knowing Christ and the power of living fully alive, Paul said, "Not that I have already obtained all this, or have already been made perfect, but I press on to take hold of that for which Christ Jesus took hold of me. Brothers, I do not consider myself yet to have taken hold of it" (Phil. 3:12–13).

The day we think we have arrived, we put one foot in the grave, part of us dies, and our ability to touch the lives of people is diminished. Remember the rocket's imperfect path to the moon? What if, halfway to its destination, the computer malfunctioned and told the rocket it had already arrived? The spacecraft would be completely without direction.

I've seen this happen when men and women retire. "I've arrived! What next?" Too often the answer is depression, loss of direction, and even death. As Anne Lamott's father, Kenneth, wrote, "[A] life oriented to leisure is in the end a life oriented to death—the greatest leisure of all."[1] I've seen it happen when people stop seeking truth because they "know it all." I've seen it happen when people lose weight, achieve physical health, and then put their lives in neutral because they have "made it." It isn't long until the weight is back. One of the early winners of *The Biggest Loser* lost more than two hundred pounds, only to gain all of it back.

Until we stand in the presence of the One who created us, we still have work to do and life to live. Paul admitted that he didn't have it all together yet because his heart was still beating and his ultimate goal was still out there—he had a strategy for living every phase of life fully alive. This strategy was the inspiration for rediscovering my spiritual life.

GET RID OF GUILT

Paul said, "I want to know Christ and the power of his resurrection. . . . Forgetting what is behind . . . I press on toward the goal" (Phil. 3:10, 13–14). Had he lived today he might have put it this way: "I want to live fully alive. So I am dropping whatever baggage is holding me back and taking only what I need to get to my goal" (Ken Davis Personal Version [KDPV]).

When Paul said, "Forgetting what is behind," he was speaking of what was behind in his own life. When you think of what he had to forget, his faith and commitment are nothing short of remarkable. As a young zealot Paul had torn apart families, persecuted and imprisoned people whose only crime was their belief in Christ. At minimum Paul was an accessory to murder.

There is one piece of baggage that not only hinders but also kills: guilt. We could empty half the psychiatric wards in this country if we could eliminate guilt. Guilt is the by-product of refusing to forget what is behind, allowing the past to stain our lives. I would rather be bedridden than guilt ridden. I have experienced both, and guilt is by far the worse pain. Hanging on to guilt is like staying in jail after you have been pardoned. Jesus took upon Himself all the guilt for every sin ever committed. He did it so that we might have a life better than we could ever imagine.

Paul experienced the forgiveness of Christ and was never the same. At every opportunity the deceiver tried to remind

Paul of the life he had lived before his conversion. If only he could crush him with guilt and a sense of worthlessness. If only he could make him believe that the horrible things he had done excluded him from experiencing the power of a holy God, excluded him from living fully alive. But Paul had been transformed. He had seen *the Light* and had his eyes set on an eternal, unshakable purpose for living. Forgetting what was behind him, refusing to carry the guilt from which Christ had set him free, Paul lived every day to take hold of a power that would sustain him in life, through persecution, and even in death. His enemies likely rejoiced at his death, but their celebration was hollow. They were blind to another celebration that ushered Paul past the grave to eternal life, where he finally tasted the ultimate power of resurrection.

One of the key aspects of knowing Christ and His power is to completely trust in the forgiveness He offers. Forgiveness. Freedom from guilt. This spiritual tenet is viable for every aspect of living fully alive. The holidays have passed and you have neglected your exercise and nutritional health for over two weeks. You have neglected your relationship with God and are missing the blessing of walking close to Him. You have intentionally sinned. Whatever we add to the list, it is always guilt that keeps us from turning back to the source of power. When the accuser brought all of Paul's past sins to mind, Paul leaned on the truth. He knew that in spite of all he had done, "because of the LORD's great love we are not consumed, for his compassions never fail. They are new every morning; great is your faithfulness" (Lam. 3:22–23). My grandson Tyler would say, "*Wow!*"

Wallowing in guilt leads to discouragement and hopelessness. In the truest sense of the word, it's a dead end. I'm not into wallowing. Occasionally I wade a little, but then I take a deep breath of His mercy and grace and get back in the race again.

DROP THE GOOD BAGGAGE

As a part of a video series titled *In Your Face*, I filmed a sequence that parodied the 1981 film *Chariots of Fire*. In the clip I'm crouched in the starting blocks, ready to run a 110-meter hurdle race. When the starting gun goes off, I explode from the blocks in slow motion and fall completely out of the frame. Suddenly I pop up and begin to run again, only to fall another time, still in slow motion. The camera pans back to reveal that I am trying to run with a bowling ball chained to my leg, and I'm dragging a huge teddy bear with me. I fall again and again. I can't run with all that baggage; I can only stumble. And when I come to the first hurdle, it really gets interesting!

This clip was filmed to set up a study of Hebrews 12, where the author confirms the very strategy Paul was endorsing. This is such great advice for any endeavor but absolutely essential for the race of life. Here's what the author said: "Let us throw off everything that hinders and the sin that so easily entangles, and let us run with perseverance the race marked out for us. Let us fix our eyes on Jesus, the author and perfecter of our faith" (Heb. 12:1–2). It's the same ultimate source of power that Paul talked about and an even more detailed strategy for getting to the finish line.

Come on! What's wrong with a teddy bear? Nothing. Except that I can't run fast lugging one around. We have only one life to live and only a given amount of energy and time to live it. If we want to live fully alive, we must make choices about how we will expend that energy and time. Any baggage in my life that keeps me from running a good race or distracts me from the ultimate objective of my life needs to be left behind. In our SCORRE conference[2] we teach communicators that any presentation has to have an objective and that anything that doesn't lead the listener to that objective needs to be eliminated from the talk.

There's a lot of baggage out there that needs to be eliminated. As much as I would like you to experience the physical benefits I've gained from consistent exercise, I would be dismayed if you allowed excessive exercise to become baggage, a detriment to your family or your walk of faith. I know people who carry religious baggage that keeps them from seriously following the Christ who holds the key to living fully alive. The author of Hebrews wasn't talking about bad baggage; he was talking about unnecessary, burdensome baggage. He was talking about good stuff that saps our energy without getting us any nearer the ultimate goal. So what's your teddy bear? The journey to living fully alive leaves a lifetime of room to enjoy many opportunities and experiences, but you can't have it all. Anything that impedes your race should be checked at the starting blocks. Sometimes the problem is the amount of baggage, not whether it's good or bad. If it's good stuff but not the right stuff, throw it!

When I was struggling to reduce the stress in my life, I told my counselor that since my last visit I had experienced several months of relief but was once again feeling anxious and unable to cope. He smiled—he always smiled—and leaned forward in his chair with his elbows on his knees, hands clasped together. "Ken," he said, "people come in here all the time carrying a lunch box full of responsibilities and worries. With medication and/or counseling I help them deal with the load they carry, and one day they leave happy and contented.

"They go home, and then because they feel so good, they throw away the lunch box, buy a suitcase, and pack it full of responsibilities, worries, and a hectic pace of life. Their suitcase is filled with so much good stuff they can't lift it. And soon they're sitting back here with me." The counseling session was over.

I realized I'd been dragging around a steamer trunk of perfectly good junk, and it was time to drop it. I traded it for the lunch box I'd carried as a kid. I'm learning to lighten up and live again. I find that I can hear God more clearly. I can see the joy in little things in life. The other day I found myself humming an old song I learned as a child, "Take Your Burden to the Lord and Leave It There." There's a reason the chorus to that little song repeats the words "leave it there" four times. We have an overwhelming tendency to take our burdens to the Lord and then drag them back home so we can pack them in a bigger trunk. Leave it! Throw it! Get rid of it!

CHUCK THE BAD BAGGAGE

Other times it's not good stuff that is dragging us down. Hebrews says, "Let us throw off everything that hinders and *the sin that so easily entangles*" (Heb. 12:1, emphasis mine). There's that old S-word that sounds so harsh to the sophisticated ear. Ignatius of Loyola, founder of the Jesuits, said, "Sin is ultimately a refusal to believe that what God wants is my happiness and fulfillment." How interesting that it's our search for that happiness in all the wrong places that keeps us from the very thing we're searching for. I have heard preachers say that God isn't concerned about our happiness. That's just not true. He is concerned that we settle for temporary pleasure when He offers ultimate joy. He offers "abundant life," and we embrace that which leads to death because it is easier and offers immediate gratification. Talk about missing the boat, falling short of the mark, living partly alive, acting like a monkey with his hand in a coconut! Years ago a camp counselor wrote in my Bible, "Sin will take you farther than you ever wanted to go, keep you longer than you ever wanted to stay, and cost you more than you ever wanted to pay." I didn't ask what the exact cost was, but I found out. Sin will stop you dead in your tracks as you seek to live fully alive. I don't need to spend a lot of time talking about this because those of us who have experienced its devastation know it's true. You can live in denial of the fact, but down deep even the most hardened person knows he can't run a good race with bad luggage tripping him up like a bowling ball chained to his leg.

The Bible promises that when we become followers of Christ and experience His forgiveness, He erases our sin from His memory. He buries it in the depths of the deepest sea. God's heart aches over the consequences of sin.

Yet on any sunny day you can find folks fishing for the very thing He died to save them from. They don't necessarily want to lug it around again. They don't think of the consequences; they only want to see it once more, maybe touch it, maybe take it home and set it on the mantel. What fools we can be! We know the consequence of sin is death but somehow convince ourselves that a little death is okay. Isn't it? No, it's not. Throw it! Get help throwing it. Ask for God's help and chuck it overboard. Forget it like He forgot it.

"FUGGEDABOUTIT"

We play games in our heads that destroy the power of life by keeping our focus away from the finish line even when we're trying to do the right thing. "I'm not going to do that thing!" we resolve as we fall asleep. Then our first waking thought in the morning is, "I'm not going to do that thing." Several times during the day we remind ourselves not to do that thing. At night we go to bed with the same resolve. "I am *not* going to do that thing." In the process, *that thing* controls us almost as securely as it did when we were doing that thing.

The amateur golfer steps up to a tee box with a water hazard lining the right side of the fairway. The first thought in his mind is, *Don't hit the ball into that thing!* Without fail the ball goes into the water because that's where he is concentrating. The pro golfer steps up to the same tee box and picks a spot down the fairway where she wants to hit the ball. Her focus is only on that spot. She doesn't even think about the water.

When Diane first started playing golf, she demonstrated a peculiar gift. Her golf balls seemed to be water-seeking missiles. She couldn't stop thinking about water hazards. If there was water anywhere on the golf course, her ball would find it. One day, after baptizing six balls, we came to a fairway without a drop of water in sight. Diane teed up with confidence and hit her best drive of the day. We watched as it soared gracefully through the air and landed—with a splash—right in the middle of the fairway.

A quick review of the scorecard confirmed it again: no water on this hole. Puzzled, we started toward Diane's ball. Reaching its landing spot, we dropped our bags and started laughing. It so happened there was a six-inch indentation in the middle of the fairway for the sprinkler system. Sitting at the bottom of this itty-bitty pool of water was Diane's ball. Now she's convinced her golf balls love water. The more determined we are to steer around something, the more likely we are to end up in the middle of it.

BRASS MONKEY PRINCIPLE

Another vivid illustration of this idea is the brass monkey principle. A college speaker taught me the lesson indelibly. "Tonight, when you go to bed," he said, "I'm asking you not to think of a brass monkey. When you pull the covers back, you may think of anything you'd like—but don't think of a brass monkey. And all day, whenever you think about going to bed, remind yourself not to think of a brass monkey."

That night when I pulled back the covers of my bed, brass monkeys were frolicking on my nightstand, perched on my lamp, and screeching and chattering beneath my pillow. They were everywhere, inescapable. Throughout the day I thought about nothing but brass monkeys.

The brass monkey principle illustrates how a problem becomes our master, rather than us mastering the problem. As a result, we make ourselves prisoners of the very things we yearn to avoid.

Have you ever said the brass monkey prayer? "I'm never going to do that *thing* again!"

Many of us say it regularly—about that very same thing. Of course, we keep doing whatever it is and eventually grow discouraged and resigned to believe that we will be doing that *thing* for the rest of our lives.

I harbor a few brass monkeys in my life. Let me tell you about one of them.

I travel more than a hundred thousand miles a year. I hold frequent-flyer status on two separate airlines. Some people believe travel is glamorous and exciting. Most of these people don't travel much. If you travel all the time, the glamour quickly wears thin. I now have luggage in major cities all over the world. They ought to hang mistletoe at each baggage check-in location—because as soon as they take possession of your stuff, you can kiss it good-bye.

I'm not proud that travel frustrations often ignite within me a less-than-gracious spirit. Translation: I can get really mean and nasty. I've been bumped from flights, I've missed connections and meetings, and I've been late getting home. On such occasions I often become . . . umm . . . unpleasant. Yet every time before I leave for an airport, I look in the mirror, lift my right hand, and say, "I won't allow myself to lose my temper. I will treat people with respect." Translation: I will not see a brass monkey.

Rather than concentrating on the behavior we should avoid, why not concentrate on the behavior we desire and on the One who can make it possible? Solomon said, "As he thinks in his heart, so is he" (Prov. 23:7 NKJV). If you're constantly thinking of that "thing," you're going to be obsessed by that "thing." Even children know that the Little Engine That Could chanted, "I think I can! I think I can!" He didn't chug up the hill puffing, "I hope I don't! I hope I don't!" In the letter to his friends in Philippi, our friend Paul said, "Forget what is behind. Ditch the guilt, the sin, the distractions, and get the monkeys off your back." That's Philippians 3:13 KDPV.

Later Paul suggested a better focus: "Finally, brothers, whatever is true, whatever is noble, whatever is right, whatever is pure, whatever is lovely, whatever is admirable—if anything is excellent or praiseworthy—think about such things. Whatever you have learned or received or heard from me, or seen in me— put it into practice. And the God of peace will be with you" (Phil. 4:8–9).

The author of Hebrews identified the best focus of all, the very source of life: "Let us run with perseverance the race marked out for us. *Let us fix our eyes on Jesus*, the author and perfecter of our faith, who for the joy set before him endured the cross, scorning its shame, and sat down at the right hand of the throne of God. Consider him who endured such opposition from sinful men, so that you will not grow weary and lose heart" (Heb. 12:1–3, emphasis mine).

If you are interested in living only partially alive, have at it.

Do the physical disciplines necessary to get in shape. Sharpen up your social skills and gather a group of supportive friends. Reach out for new opportunities and resolve to never stop learning. I promise you your life will be better for the trying. But if you want to live fully alive, then accept the gift of forgiveness offered by the Creator of the universe, and don't look back.

Have you decided to forget what is behind? Are you going to bring with you only what will fit under your seat and in the overhead compartment? What's next?

Chapter Twelve

THE SOURCE

BY THE TIME I PREPARED MY FIRST TALK ABOUT LIVING fully alive, I had already begun my physical transformation. I started feeling the benefits almost immediately. However, I longed for more than just physical fitness. The needle on my spiritual gas tank registered empty. I hadn't lost my faith; my faith had atrophied for lack of exercise. I had stopped risking and trusting. I was comfortable.

Deep within us is a God-given desire to live. I can remember from my childhood camp speakers who tried to persuade us to make a commitment of faith by using variations of the following appeal: "If you were to die tonight, where would you spend eternity?" I appreciated the challenge. After all, eternity is a long time, and the hope of eternal life is an important element of faith. But there was another equally important question that was rarely addressed. What if I live? What will faith in Christ bring to the quality of my life right now? I was prepared for death. I wanted to be prepared for life. Jesus Himself said He came to give us life in abundance. I wanted a piece of that action.

I now wanted to experience a renewal of spiritual courage and faith like the one I was experiencing physically. I wasn't ready for a spiritual triathlon, but my soul yearned to run again. I wanted to feel the wind in my face and experience sore muscles as evidence of spiritual growth.

Okay, I know some of you are tempted to skip this part. *Don't do it!* Even if the idea of spiritual growth doesn't appeal to you, this was the most important and most difficult leg of my journey to living fully alive. Please listen to this part of my story.

THE SPIRITUAL SCALES OF MY LIFE

One morning I sat over a cup of coffee with my friend Bob Stromberg. I had lost forty pounds and several pants sizes over the past months, but I was troubled about what I saw when I stepped on the spiritual scales of my life. As I waited for my coffee to cool a bit, I asked Bob a question I'd been asking myself. "How has your life changed in the past few years because of the power of Christ living in you?" We both stared at the steam rising from our cups. Change and growth are signs of life. I had felt the snow stinging my face and had accepted the physical challenge to live fully alive. Now I wanted a sled ride for my spirit.

Finally I confessed to Bob that I couldn't identify even a single aspect of my life that had changed in the last month. I couldn't identify any growth in the last year. Come on! I travel the world challenging people to become followers of Jesus. Was it possible that as people listened and watched me for signs of life they could see none? Could I accidentally be pronounced spiritually dead? Of course I had the hope of eternal life, but earthly life is not a waiting room for eternal life. I needed a taste of it now.

What had happened? When had I stopped growing? Where was the adventure? I had no battle wounds, bloodstains, or scars because I had fought no battles and had won no victories. I had grown comfortable in my career, comfortable with my life, and comfortable with my faith. But I felt little joy in it. There's a big difference between comfort and joy. A comfortable faith is no faith at all.

That day I cried out to God, "Lord, I want to renew the joy of my salvation. I want to mount up on wings like eagles. I want to fly again. I don't want to be just physically alive; I want to be fully alive." The very nature of the words *fully alive* implies completeness. We are physical, social, mental, and spiritual beings. To ignore any aspect of our humanity is to be only partially alive. I'm not interested in partial life any more than I'm interested in partial plates or premature death.

A comfortable life is not the path to being fully alive. It's a ticket to boredom and despair. That's why I run and swim and walk and play exhausting games of racquetball. It's why I set out to be younger next year. I want to race and risk, and I want to go to bed at night with a prayer on my lips—the same prayer I prayed after crashing in the snow bank. *God, thank You. I am alive. Not just living, but alive!*

I went back to examine more closely Paul's desire to live fully alive. At first I had concentrated on the power. Show me the money! My faith, my life, my hope, everything rests on the belief that Christ was raised from the dead. I can't think of a more dramatic or important miracle. It's one of the central elements of faith. If Jesus is dead, we who believe in Him are fools. But He's alive, so give me some of that power! The first time around, though, I had missed something. In his declaration, Paul actually expressed a desire to know *two* things. And they both come in the same package. You can't have one without the other. Paul said, "I want to know *Christ* and *the power of his resurrection*" (Phil. 3:10, emphasis mine).

There it was. In that sentence lay the secret to knowing the power of Christ's resurrection. It is tied directly to knowing *Him*. Hello! Once again, relationship trumps religious formula. But wait! As a child I had learned of Paul's dramatic conversion. Didn't he already know Christ?

Of course the answer is yes. Paul was a believer, but he wanted an even deeper relationship. He wasn't satisfied to know about Christ; he wanted to know the full extent of His love and grace. The power to live fully alive comes from knowing Christ better. From the beginning of time, He has been the source of life: "Through him all things were made; without him nothing was made that has been made. In him was life, and that life was the light of men" (John 1:3–4).

That is the source of the growth Bob and I had discussed. Becoming better is far more than fulfilling a bunch of resolutions. It's more than a systematic attempt at behavior management. It's a natural outcome of knowing Christ better.

But how do I do that? I know how to know Bob Stromberg better. We spend time over hot coffee; we talk and listen to one another. I allow him to challenge me. I know how to know my wife better. I find ways to demonstrate my love for her. I spend time with her. I share my innermost thoughts with her. But how do I know God better? Pretty much the same way.

I must confess I had grown to take my Creator, my Savior, for granted. I didn't spend much time with Him anymore. I was so busy encouraging other people to begin a relationship with Him that I had neglected the most important relationship in my own life. I spent very little time reading the record of who He is and how much He loves me. I was too busy to read and allow His Spirit to talk to me. I was telling other people to trust a God whom I hadn't spent time with for a long while.

AN INTIMATE RELATIONSHIP WITH THE SOURCE

Shortly after making a commitment to deepen my relationship with Christ, I was asked to preach at one of the largest churches in the country. I was gratified by the invitation, but in light of my spiritual renewal, I knew this would be a special message. I wanted it to be more than a performance. Because of the significance of what God was doing in my life, I wanted to challenge these people to new life. I don't know if I had ever worked harder to prepare a message.

Finally the Sunday arrived. It was a day I will never forget. I was told that there would be baptisms preceding my message. It wasn't until the announcements that I realized there would be seventy-five baptisms! No wonder there was such a huge tank of water on the platform.

Quickly I did the calculations. Even if each baptism took only a minute there would be over an hour of baptisms! Certainly this would shorten my message. How could I bless people with my important message if I had to condense it? Maybe I could challenge them to live partially alive. How quickly the human heart darts from the right path. What happened in the next minutes changed my life.

It was a well-organized service. I watched as several pastors baptized people at the same time. Sometimes entire families who had come to know Christ were baptized together. The importance of my carefully prepared message slid to the back burner without me being aware of it. God was using this occasion to deliver a deeper and more profound message of His power. Men and women and children emerged from the water with tears of joy streaming from their faces. One couple, whose marriage had been salvaged by the power of Christ's love, stood sopping wet after being baptized, clinging to one another in gratitude for their newfound love. There was no rush to get them out of the tank. There was only an overwhelming sense of joy. The notes to my message slipped to the floor. The worship team singing perfect songs to fit this moment disappeared. The aisles of the church were filled with family and friends there to show their support and love. All played a supporting role to faces that shined with supernatural evidence of a new life.

Near the end of the baptisms, a young boy who appeared to be in his early teens stepped into the water alone. His chubby young face beamed as the pastor whispered instructions and asked for his confession of faith. The boy nodded. He was baptized in the name of the Father, the Son, and the Holy Spirit and declared to all present the source of his joy. As he emerged from the water, I saw her. An elderly woman juggling a camera and a cane was weeping openly as she struggled to navigate the crowded aisle so she could get a picture of this boy, her grandson. Two of us jumped up to help her get the picture. Her grandson had seen her and waited eagerly at the edge of the baptismal for her to snap the photo. "Thank you," she whispered as we handed her camera back. "This is the best day of my life."

I squeezed her hand. "It's one of the best days of my life too."

After that service I called Bob Stromberg. I reminded him of the question I had asked at the coffee shop about evidence of spiritual growth in our lives. "I changed today," I said. "I'm still alive!"

"That's great!" he said with sincere enthusiasm. "Take two more of whatever you had and call me in the morning." That was Bob's way of saying he couldn't talk right then. I reported to him the next day that I hadn't taken any drugs. I had watched the power of Christ's resurrection reflected in the faces of seventy-five people. You never see the same expressions when people clutch the keys to a new car or cash a lottery check. These were deeper, more powerful expressions. They are filled with hope and significance and redemption and love. I had been so concerned about my sermon, yet by the end of that morning if they had simply asked me to close with prayer I would have been happy. If the only contribution I had made was to take a picture to record the greatest day in a grandmother's life, I would have been happy. A little over a year later, I would have the privilege of baptizing two of my grandsons, Bailey and Preston. What a thrill to proclaim, "Buried in the likeness of his death and raised to newness of life." That day I whispered in their ears, "Live, boys, live!"

I baptized Bailey, the youngest, first and asked him to wait in the corner of the baptismal until I finished with his brother. He didn't wait. Bailey dived beneath the water just as I dunked his brother Preston. I could see his eyes bulging under the water. When he came to the surface, Bailey whispered, "I just wanted to see it close up, Grandpa." My sentiments exactly. I want to see the glory of God close up. God reminded me that day that it was time to follow my own advice and move toward a more intimate relationship with the Source of resurrection power.

I remember the story of a farmer driving to the market with his wife. Halfway there she turned to him and said, "How come we don't sit close together no more like we did when we was first married?" Without taking his eyes from the road, the farmer clutched the steering wheel a bit tighter and responded, "I ain't moved." He had always driven the car. It was his wife who had moved.

The spiritual dryness I had felt wasn't God's fault. He hadn't moved; I had. I had stopped taking time to be with Him, to learn of Him, to find ways to express my love to Him. I had stopped looking for His presence in the little things of life. If I was to live fully alive, I needed to renew my friendship with the Creator of life.

BREATH OF LIFE

Watching the sunrise from a perch high in the mountains reminded me of the Source of power. It was a gorgeous dawn as we started up the mountain trail. Glimpses of the valley below flashed briefly between the alpine trees. Farther up the trail and a thousand feet higher, we were surrounded by pine and aspen groves, immersed in the fragrance of a mountain forest, savoring the gift of unique and wonderful aromas. It was a bracing, exhilarating climb, filled with sweet memories of other times on the trail. But there was a nagging sensation that something was missing.

Two hours later we were above timberline at thirteen thousand feet. The entire valley lay in splendor below us, and hazy mountaintops guarded the distant horizon. The sky was crystal clear. I could see for a hundred miles. Suddenly I knew what was missing: oxygen. I had a great view of that clear, serene sky because I was lying flat on my back, gasping for breath. The top of the mountain beckoned to me, but my lungs said, "Forget the top of the mountain—find something to breathe!" I knew where the oxygen was, and it wasn't up. It was down, near the trees and rabbits and other living things. I have a friend who has climbed Mt. Whitney and another who has scaled all fifty-four peaks in Colorado more than fourteen thousand feet. I didn't care. All I wanted were lungs full of really excellent air—or much, much bigger lungs.

As I lay there, I remembered that when I was earning my pilot's license, I really didn't believe oxygen was that important. The regulations require that it be used any time a pilot is flying an unpressurized aircraft above ten thousand feet for more than a half hour. Above twelve thousand feet oxygen is required at all times. I had flown at those altitudes many times without any noticeable effects. I'm a big boy. I've lived thirty years at fifty-five hundred feet. I've climbed above thirteen thousand feet many times. Why would I need oxygen?

One moonless night my flight instructor strapped me in an airplane and told me to climb to ten thousand feet and level off. All the way up he reviewed the regulations on oxygen use. I leveled off at ten thousand feet and he said, "Look at your instrument panel." Thinking this was part of some test to see if I could spot a faulty instrument reading, I stared at the panel but could see nothing wrong. What was I missing? The instructor reached in the back seat and grabbed an oxygen mask. "Keep looking at the panel," he commanded. My mind raced. Had I misread the regulation? I wasn't required to use oxygen because we'd only been at this altitude for a few minutes.

As I stared at the panel, he turned on the oxygen and placed the mask over my nose and mouth. Suddenly the panel lights were turned to full bright. They were so bright I had to blink my eyes. He hadn't touched the control. It was oxygen. Without it, my ability to see had been significantly impaired. Had I stayed at that altitude longer, my vision would have deteriorated even more. Without enough oxygen, vision is impaired. At higher altitudes a person who is deprived of oxygen loses the ability to do simple math or make life-and-death decisions. Without oxygen, there is no vision. Where there is no vision, the people perish.

Exhausted Super Bowl players sit on a bench and suck down pure oxygen. It's their source of renewed power and strength. At the risk of sounding simplistic, knowing Christ is not only the source of our power and strength but also the source of life.

That Sunday at the baptism I dove for the oxygen. I heard again the words of Bob Thompson: "Live what you say you believe, son! You can do this." I was even lazier and more out of shape spiritually than I was physically. That conversation with Bob Stromberg was The "Noooooo!" Photo of my spiritual condition.

Fortunately, although we may neglect God or even give up on Him, He never gives up on us. God was there at the wild sled ride. He was there nudging me to take a second look at The Manatee Photo. He was there at the baptism pointing to the right path for me. And as I began to take time to know Him again, to read of His love and grace, to listen for the direction He wanted for my life, He was there. I started to experience His power in my life again. I began to sense His presence. Seek power by itself, and you will die searching. Seek to know Christ, and He will show you His resurrection power. That was the day I set out with renewed intensity to know better the One who could lead me to live fully alive. I would soon discover that Paul left even further instructions that would help me find my way.

Chapter Thirteen

PRESS ON

SO HERE WE STAND, STRIPPED OF THE BAGGAGE THAT WILL keep us from running a good race, wondering, "What do I do next?" Paul says, "Get moving! Keep pressing toward the goal." It does no good to put on running shorts and tennis shoes if you never get out of the starting blocks. In other words, move!

I remember an elderly missionary who spoke at my alma mater, Oak Hills Bible College. Long after many of his friends had retired, he was still living fully alive. His name disappeared from my brain long ago, but I have never forgotten his message.

"Most Christians," he began, "have moss growing on their butts!" There was a collective audible gasp from the audience. The word *butt* had probably never been spoken in that chapel before. But it was obvious he was not trying to be funny. He continued in a grave tone.

"The moss grows because we sit in the pews our entire lives, crying out to God, 'If You want me to do something for You, open a door, and I will respond.'"

He was so right. I had spent significant time praying for God to open doors in my life. Then, with a twinkle in his eye, this amazing man continued. "My life has been filled with excitement and adventure. I have trusted that God was calling me to His service and would not let me down. I've used common sense and prayer as preparation. But I refuse to sit still. I'm at full throttle, aiming at the next project, crying out to God, 'Lord, if You don't want me in there, shut the door!'"

Then he smiled for the first time, turned his back to us, and exclaimed, "Look! There's no moss growing on my butt!" Indeed there wasn't.

So stand up! Fix your eyes on the goal, start moving, and keep moving. It's important to remember that the throwing-off exercise—or perhaps a better word is *exorcise*—is a continual part of staying fully alive. A rolling stone may gather no moss, but human beings pick up a variety of junk even while on the move. Keep throwing off the garbage that accumulates and run toward the goal of knowing "Christ and the power of His resurrection." All the energy is focused on running *toward* the very Power that sustains the universe.

Don't be discouraged if you have to breathe hard. Don't give up if life seems like a battle. It is! If you can't smell gunpowder or feel pain, if you never fall or accumulate junk that needs to be tossed, you are "fully dead." That's opposite from the direction you want to be going. Press on.

BANISH FEAR

Since we're talking about garbage, I would like you to do a little exercise as a part of reading this chapter. Relax. You can do this one sitting down.

Write the word *fear* at the bottom of a sheet of paper. Write it tiny and in lowercase letters. Now at the top of the page write the word *confidence*. Put that one in large capital letters. Go back down to the bottom of the page, just above that tiny word *fear*. Write down all the things you're afraid of: failure, rejection, looking foolish, losing a job, illness.

Get them out there. Write them all in small lowercase letters. All those fears are like nasty little vampires that can suck the joy and energy from life. If we let them into our lives, they have the capacity to keep us from pressing on and taking hold of the adventure God has waiting for us.

There is a reason I have asked you to write your fears at the bottom of the paper in tiny letters. They cannot and will not be our main focus. To concentrate on your fears would be as silly as concentrating on brass monkeys. Instead, copy the words of Psalm 23 beneath the word *confidence* at the top of the page. I know you can simply read the psalm in your Bible, but there is something about writing a thought down that cements it in your brain. Write boldly. I'll wait.

> The Lord is my shepherd, I shall not be in want.
> He makes me lie down in green pastures,
>   he leads me beside quiet waters,
>   he restores my soul.
> He guides me in paths of righteousness
>   for his name's sake.
> Even though I walk
>   through the valley of the shadow of death,
>   I will fear no evil,
>   for you are with me;
>   your rod and your staff,
>   they comfort me.

> You prepare a table before me
>> in the presence of my enemies.
> You anoint my head with oil;
>> my cup overflows.
> Surely goodness and love will follow me
>> all the days of my life,
> and I will dwell in the house of the LORD
>> forever.

Did you happen to have "walking through the valley of the shadow of death" written as one of your fears? There is no scarier place. That is the ultimate place of fear. All other fears bow down to "walking through the valley of the shadow of death." In that valley it is difficult to stand, let alone press on. I have committed to read the Twenty-third Psalm every morning for the rest of my life. I want to read it before any fear can grab my attention. What confidence to know that my faith is in the only One who conquered death and gave me that same power to live my life.

I love old vampire movies. Wait! I saw that frown. Stay with me here. There's an important point to be made. The old classics portrayed a message of hope that is missing in the dark, graphic vampire films of today. Of course I don't believe there are such things as vampires. Even if there were, they would be no threat to any person of average intelligence. Simply avoid people who hiss, don't talk to anyone who doesn't have a reflection, and don't ever say to anyone, "Bite me!" I hear it also helps to eat lots of garlic. Common sense stuff. Here's why I love the old movies. They leave no doubt that if you really want to be safe from a vampire, never go anywhere without a cross. Unlike the dark, hopeless films of today, the old features acknowledged the power associated with the cross. A lone person could hold off a horde of vampires simply by lifting up the cross. The flesh of the vampire would burn when it came in contact with the cross. Evil could not conquer in the presence of the cross.

There are no real vampires, but as you press on, "vampires" that are capable of sucking the joy and adventure out of living fully alive will line your path. Fear is the daddy of them all. Temptation and idolatry and a host of other children make up the rest of the family. Three things are important to remember:

1. These vampires are exceptional liars.
2. Their only mission is to destroy.
3. The power of the cross and the resurrection exceeds anything they can throw your direction.

What happened on the cross took the sting from the most hideous monster of all. More than conquering "the valley of the shadow of death," it took the sting from death itself, as 1 Corinthians proclaims so joyfully: "'Where, O death, is your victory? Where, O death, is your sting?' The sting of death is sin, and the power of sin is the law. But thanks be to God! He gives us the victory through our Lord Jesus Christ" (1 Cor. 15:55–57).

Absolutely nothing can separate me from the love of God that is in Christ. I can press forward in confidence even when I have to walk through the darkest valley. The Bible assures us, "The one who is in you is greater than the one who is in the world" (1 John 4:4). The spirit of fear is in-*fear*-ior to the Spirit of Christ who lives in us.

It's time for me to confess that much of my life was ruled by fear. When I began my journey to living fully alive, I tried everything to help vanquish fear. Counseling helped, and I'm thankful for the medication that helped, but the greatest victory over fear came as I learned to risk my life for His sake—a far greater adventure than a wild ride in a shallow bathtub.

RISK IT ALL

Pressing on is about taking risks based on God's promises of power rather than missing out on life because of your fear of—you name it. I'm serious. Write your fear right here in the margin.The road from that fear to confidence is called risk. Risk is the demonstration of faith.

When my daughter Traci was a little girl, I found her standing on the landing of the courthouse steps, staring at the ground. She was only about seven feet from the ground, but that's a long fall for a little girl. So I walked to a spot below where she stood to make sure she didn't hurt herself. "Daddy, I want to jump!" she said. "Will you catch me?" (Traci is now the mother of four of my grandchildren.)

"Jump," I said. "I'll catch you."

"No, I'm scared."

"Don't worry, I'll catch you."

"Will you really catch me?"

"Yes, I promise."

"Okay!"

We counted to three. We counted to ten. We counted backward from ten. We said, "Get ready! Get set! Go!" Each time, at the point of commitment, she would back away and ask for reassurance.

"You *will* catch me?"

She moved toward the edge again. "What's wrong?" I asked.

She said, "My rear end feels funny." I explained that risk always makes your rear end feel funny.

Then, finally, Traci did what God wants us to do. She leaned so far forward that she couldn't turn back. Notice I didn't say that she backed off, got a run at it, and leaped fearlessly into the air. This was no huge demonstration of bravery; it was a tiny move of faith. How much faith does it take for a little girl to jump into her daddy's arms? Enough faith to lean forward (the key word is *forward*) just far enough so she can't turn back. As she tumbled, a scream tore from her throat, but the second she hit my arms everything changed. Her expression changed from one of fear to one of delight, and the first words out of her mouth were, "Let's do it again!" She squirmed from my arms, and before I knew it she was back on the landing. With each jump she grew more confident. In the end she was throwing herself with abandon from the landing into my arms. By risking, Traci had moved from fear to confidence, and along the way she had learned to trust her dad.

That's what God wants to do for us. Faith is taking the risk to put your life on the line for what you say you believe. God doesn't always ask you to take breathtaking leaps from a courthouse landing, but He does ask you to lean forward. People who stop taking risks stop living.

It's amazing how confidence grows once we are willing to risk. Will it hurt? Occasionally. But it will be worth it. When your ultimate hope is in something bigger than death itself, then fear has to take a backseat to living.

When I first started riding my bicycle in Tennessee, I wore out my brakes. If it was a brutal physical challenge trying to make it up Yardstick Hill, it was a terrifying mental challenge to go down Yardstick Hill without touching the brakes. After several weeks of riding up and down that hill, I became so confident that I was grinding my way up the hill several times each ride just so I could experience the thrill of flying back down as fast as I could go. "Daddy, let's do it again!" One day I rocketed down Yardstick Hill without touching the brakes. My speedometer recorded my max speed at fifty-one miles per hour.

I can testify that hitting a Tennessee June bug at fifty-one miles per hour is like hitting a small horse, especially when you factor in the speed of the June bug.

When I told Diane of my adventure, she scolded me. "Honey, you're only one acorn away from death," she warned. That spooked me a little. The next time I rode down that hill, when I wasn't dodging June bugs my eyes were bugging out of my head scanning the road for acorns. If you can't see a June bug, you can't see an acorn. But I tried. That's why I didn't see the stupid dog.

He tore at full speed from a hidden driveway, snarling and barking. He startled me so badly that I jerked the handlebars, which made the front wheel of my bike begin to oscillate violently back and forth. I thought the bicycle was going to disintegrate right out from under me. The only way to stop that kind of vibration is to apply the brakes. But a vicious dog was closing in behind me. I glanced back and saw a foaming mouth and bared teeth.

That's when I hit the acorn.

I left skin on the asphalt that day, but even as I slid along the ground, I knew I was fully alive. When I stopped sliding those were the first words out of my mouth. "Thank God I'm alive!" The second words out of my mouth were, "Where's the dog?" I never saw him again. I can only guess that one look at me in spandex biking shorts with half my skin gone was more than he could handle.

Now before you head for the garage to dust off your old Schwinn, understand that you don't need to ride a bike down a hill at breakneck speeds to be fully alive. But if you intend to live fully alive, you must realize that it will involve risk and you will hit acorns of your own. As you reach out socially you will risk rejection, as you start to get in shape physically there will be injuries, and spiritual growth is certainly not without setbacks and pain.

Banish fear from your life. God has promised to be with you. Take risks in the face of each of those fears written on the bottom of the paper and discover *confidence*.

Risk by reaching out to people who may reject you.

Risk by trying things you have never tried before.

Risk by giving until it hurts.

Risk by following the steps of Christ no matter what the cost.

Risk by forgiving when your heart prefers to clutch bitterness.

Risk by taking the first step of faith by trusting Christ.

Risk by tossing off all the stuff that hinders.

Risk by asking God for the strength to toss out sin that is tripping you up.

Risk by committing to a program of diet and exercise that will lead to health.

Risk by looking for opportunity to serve.

THE LAW OF THE PENDULUM

In college I was asked to deliver a persuasive speech that would convince people to believe a propositional truth. We would be graded on our creativity, persuasiveness, and ability to drive home a point in a memorable way. The title of my talk was "The Law of the Pendulum." I spent twenty minutes carefully teaching the physical principles that govern a swinging pendulum. I taught that a pendulum can never return to a point higher than the point from which it was released. Because of friction and gravity, a swinging pendulum will fall short of its original position. Each time it swings it creates a shorter arc, until finally it is at rest. This point of rest is called the state of equilibrium, where all forces acting on the pendulum are equal and it ceases to move.

I attached a three-foot string to a child's toy top and thumbtacked it to the top of the blackboard. I pulled the toy to one side and made a mark on the blackboard where I let it go. Each time it swung back I made a new mark. It took only a short time for the top to complete its swinging and come to rest. When I finished the demonstration, the markings on the blackboard proved my thesis.

I then asked how many people in the room believed the law of the pendulum was true. All of my classmates raised their hands, and so did the professor. Believing I had finished my demonstration, he started to walk to the front of the room. In reality, it had just begun.

Hanging from the steel ceiling beams in the middle of the room was a large crude but functional pendulum: 250 pounds of metal weights taped together and tied to four strands of 500-pound-test parachute cord. Sitting against the wall on one end of the room was a table with a chair on top of it. I invited the instructor to climb up on the table and sit in the chair with the back of his head against the cement wall. Then I brought the 250 pounds of metal up to his nose. Holding the huge pendulum just a fraction of an inch from his face, I once again explained the law of the pendulum he had applauded only moments before.

"If the law of the pendulum is true," I said, "then when I release this mass of metal, it will swing across the room and return short of the release point. Your nose and face will be in no danger." After that final restatement of this law, I looked him in the eye and asked, "Sir, do you believe this law is true?"

There was a long pause. Beads of sweat formed on his upper lip, and then weakly he nodded and whispered, "Yes."

I released the pendulum. It made a soft swishing sound as

it arced across the room. At the far end of its swing, it paused momentarily and started back. I never saw a man move so fast in my life. The professor literally dived from the table. Deftly stepping around the still-swinging pendulum, I asked the class, "Does he believe in the law of the pendulum?"

The students unanimously answered, "*No!*"

He believed it intellectually, but he was unwilling to trust his nose to it. One of the most fascinating and unexpected outcomes of the lesson was that another student volunteered to sit in the chair. Though he flinched when the pendulum swung toward his face, he stayed put. Once the students saw the validity of the law demonstrated, they all wanted to do it. The desire to live out demonstrated faith is not only adventurous; it's contagious.[1]

If you're wired like me, it's time to pump up the tires on that old bike and find yourself a Yardstick Hill. Most of all, it's time to *risk* by getting to know Christ. Read the record He left for us. Study His promises. Listen for the prompting of His Spirit, and then act. Live out the faith you say you believe. Lean out so far you can't turn back, and discover that He can be trusted. It won't be long before you begin to shout, "Let's do it again!"

The author of Hebrews has challenged us to throw off sin and the garbage that hinders us: "Therefore, since we are surrounded by such a great cloud of witnesses, let us throw off everything that hinders and the sin that so easily entangles, and let us run with perseverance the race marked out for us" (Heb. 12:1). Those witnesses were the incredible heroes of faith listed in chapter 11 of Hebrews. I found great motivation and inspiration reading of these imperfect but committed people. Read Hebrews 11 for yourself. Those men and women risked everything for what they believed. They couldn't even see the finish line from where they stood, but they held on to the little knowledge they had and ran full speed ahead. You and I have sound evidence and a reliable record that Jesus has risen from the dead and that He is coming again. We have the promise of eternal life. We have no reason to hold anything back.

As a friend told me not long ago, "Whenever you have an important decision to make, ask yourself this: What would you do if you weren't afraid? That's usually the answer you need."

Okay, let's finish our word exercise. Find that paper with the words *fear* and *confidence* written on it. Now, rip the page in half. Keep the top half with the word *confidence* and the Twenty-third Psalm written on it. In the true spirit of forgetting what is behind, burn the bottom half of the page with *fear* written on it as confirmation of your commitment to live fully alive.

Then lean forward and risk it all.

Chapter Fourteen

OUT OF THE VALLEY OF
THE SHADOW OF DEATH

SAILORS KEEP A LOG OF THE EVENTS AND COURSE CHANGES
the entire time they're at sea. Racers keep a record of their times
so they can see if they're improving. Pilots follow a predeter-
mined path on a GPS and record even their conversations to
analyze the safety and efficiency of their cockpit performance.

When I read the Twenty-third Psalm and the promises of
God, I see them as records of His faithfulness. The whole Bible
is, in fact, a record of God's love and faithfulness. I don't know
where I would be without that record.

LOGGING THE LEGACY

Keep a record of your journey on the path to living fully alive.
You can do it on a computer if you wish, but I use small notebooks bound with leather. They smell better than my computer.

I make notes of where I've been and where I'm headed. I write down thoughts and ideas that drop in at odd hours of the day. I keep track of my workouts and the food I eat. I write down the e-mail addresses of new friends. However, when I forget to take one of the notebooks out of my pocket and Diane runs it through the wash, all that's left is a pathetic remnant of tattered pages with blotches of ink. I would rather lose a hundred-dollar bill than ruin one of those books. That's the only reason I'm considering keeping a digital record of my journey. Diane has never accidently washed my computer.

Occasionally I sketch a picture of an event or person that affected my life. None of these will ever hang in a museum, but they're priceless to me. My record is spotty and has some huge gaps in it, yet like a trail of bread crumbs, the words lead to evidence of God's hand in my life. While following those crumbs, I find hidden stakes I missed the first time around.

One Valentine's Day I bought several of those soft, nice-smelling little notebooks for my grandchildren. The older children immediately sat down and started writing. Since Jadyn (you remember Jadyn, my mountain explorer) couldn't read or write yet, I was worried she might feel left out. My fears were put to rest as I watched her carefully open her journal. She put the pencil to her lips like she was thinking of what to write. Then, as if some important thought had suddenly occurred to her, she began to scribble and muttered, "Dear Diarrhea!" The entire house erupted in laughter. I hope those beloved children experience the benefits of keeping a record of their journeys for years to come.

Some people say, "What's the big deal? I'll write it all down when I get older." Trust me, when you get older you won't even be able to remember where you put your pen. If you write daily, you will capture thoughts and ideas that otherwise would disappear, leaving only a vague hint of some brilliant concept that could save the planet. I learned the hard way to write out my thoughts in complete sentences. I woke up one night with a profound thought dancing in my head. The concept was so revolutionary I couldn't sleep. I turned on the light and reached for a tablet I keep on the nightstand. Once the idea was on paper I quickly drifted off to sleep. The next morning I grabbed the notebook to review the earth-shattering thought that had kept me awake. Scrawled across the top of the paper was the word *chicken*. Chicken? I had no idea what it meant or how chicken could save the planet. Don't wait until you're older. Remember your Creator in the days of your youth because when you're old, *everything* will depart from you.

THE VALLEY

In going back through my journals for this book, I read an entry made at one of the lowest points in my life. This was during a time when I struggled with debilitating depression. Reading that entry drove me to my knees in thanks to God for the full life I'm living today. I was instantly reminded of how His grace surrounded me and brought me out of that pit to the level of joy I have today. I debated whether to share this entry, but I have no choice. It is Exhibit A confirming the power of Christ's resurrection and how it changed my life. Here's the entry I wrote almost ten years ago:

> *Friday*—I am paralyzed. Going through the motions without life. A zombie. The glimmer of hope seems so small compared to the weight of my sin and pain. Am I Judas? Am I Peter? I don't know which one I will emulate in the end.
>
> I pray for joy. I pray for the cleansing of grace.
>
> I can't see tomorrow from here. Yet I must plan for it.

I feel like I am trying to build a house with the almost certain knowledge it will be destroyed. It is difficult to find the strength to drive the smallest nail. It is impossible to carry a heavy load of lumber. Any moment of joy at seeing the house take shape is quickly torn to shreds by the vision of its destruction. The blueprints are covered with blood. Not just the blood of (me) the builder but all those who labored with him. And those who saw the hope of shelter within the walls.

My bones are weary. My strength is gone. I can do nothing to dispel the darkness that slowly envelops me. I will not curse God. It is myself that I curse. That I cannot feel His presence is my fault. I have built walls that are impenetrable. Not impenetrable by God but by me.

I long to see His face, to hear His voice. I long for His comfort. I am undone.

I have smelled the stench of death. It does not attract me. I am repelled by it. But wherever I turn the stench is there. My only prayer is for but a glimpse of His face. A ray of hope. Please God. Please.

Very few people knew of the depth of my struggle during that time. Those who did would later ask what I did to find my way out of such a pit. The *only* thing I did was lean toward God. I cried out to Him like a seaweed-covered prophet in the belly of a fish. And as with Jonah, God heard my cry. I felt like I couldn't get to God, but He got to me. He was my only hope. When I wrote that entry, no medication or counseling had been able to stop the emotional spiral that kept me from sleeping or getting out of bed. (What a conundrum: What good is it to be trapped in bed if you can't sleep?) During those horrible days, fear reigned, and the deceiver reminded me of every sin I had ever committed and hissed like that malevolent PE instructor long ago: "You will never amount to anything! You are worthless. Follow the path of Judas. End it!" His deceptive lie was the exact opposite of the hope I live and write about today. His call was a call to death. But then God intervened.

In my anguish I begged, "God, where are You?" I guess I expected to see Him standing at the foot of my bed. But He revealed Himself in other ways. My sister flew across the country and sat by my side for days, held my hand, and prayed. She reminded me of God's promises and pointed to things like a shaft of sunlight streaming through the skylight and a blooming flower as evidence of God's existence and love. Her honest but unshakable faith and her love for me fanned within me the smoldering desire to live. I had asked, "God, where are You?" He had never left. As I read the record of my sister's visit and see her encouraging words, I can hear a stake being tapped into the ground. Tap. Tap. Can you hear it?

One morning I prayed, "Lord, give me a sign!" That day I met a counselor who looked like a cross between Burl Ives and Santa Claus and had the heart of a saint. No Sigmund Freud frown on this face—it radiated a passion to show people the grace of God and to restore hope to their lives. He pointed out teddy bears, bowling balls, and chains of oppression I had dragged with me for years. I must have looked like the back end of the car driven by newlyweds. He gently coaxed me to loosen my grip on all the junk I had lugged around for years and encouraged me to run, to press on, to live. Could the loving counsel of this saint be a sign? Tap. Tap. Tap. Another stake went in.

My journals reveal stake after stake that identified God's gentle guidance back to the land of the living. One day I wrote, "I can see colors again. The world is no longer shades of gray. Storm clouds threaten, but they are gilded with Light, evidence that above them the Son still shines." On another day I wrote, "I was drowning. My strength was gone. The harder I tried to make it to shore, the harder the tide fought me. Then I felt my toe touch the sand. Praise God! A foothold! I'm not out of the water yet, but I'm going to make it." I still share one entry in my journal with people who've been discouraged by unthinking people who criticize them for taking medication to aid their battle with depression: "Thank God for chemistry!"

Be encouraged. This road to life is punctuated with potholes and setbacks. If you've experienced some bumps along the way, it's evidence that you're alive. There will be days when you can't see the sun. Don't despair.

Years after my recovery, I started to let fear get the best of me again. I was afraid I might be headed back to the darkness. How interesting. I wasn't depressed; I was afraid of *becoming* depressed. Instead of leaning forward, I shrank backward, embracing that old fear like some idiot opening the window to let a nasty bat bite him in the neck. Franklin D. Roosevelt said, "The only thing we have to fear is fear itself." He wasn't a theologian, but he was right.

My three granddaughters were staying with us the night I decided it was time to visit with my counselor, Burl Ives/Santa Claus, again. I needed help. One is a lonely number, but by now I had a team of friends and professionals who loved me and made themselves available. We bundled three sleepy girls into the back of the car and pulled onto the highway. Because they were so young, we had never spoken to them about what I had been through in the past or was feeling at the present. Halfway to our destination, a tiny voice piped up from the backseat. It was Jadyn again. (Who else would it be?) The little girl who a year later would get lost in the mountains. "I think we need to pray for Grandpa," she said. She forced her sisters to hold hands and then prayed this prayer.

"Please, God, don't let my grandpa be afraid."

Pause.

"Help him think of bunnies and rainbows and happy faces."

Long pause.

"Please, God, don't let my grandpa forget about Jesus."

Pause.

"All the men." (Her version of "amen.")

From the mouths of babes! A three-year-old uttered words of hope that would become the foundation of my healing. The clouds parted. I could see the Son again. The very next day I was waiting at the airport for a delayed flight when my cell phone rang. On the line was the unmistakable voice of my friend Chonda Pierce. She had just published *Laughing in the Dark*, an account of her own battle with depression, and was aware of what I had faced years before. But she knew nothing of the struggle I was facing now. "Hello, have you got time for me to read you something?" I would have answered, but Chonda rarely gives opportunity for an answer. "Listen to this." She continued:

> Don't be afraid, I've redeemed you.
>   I've called your name. You're mine.
> When you're in over your head, I'll be there with you.
>   When you're in rough waters, you will not go down.
> When you're between a rock and a hard place,
>   it won't be a dead end—
> Because I am God, your personal God,
>   The Holy of Israel, your Savior.
> I paid a huge price for you:
>   all of Egypt, with rich Cush and Seba thrown in!
> That's how much you mean to me!
>   That's how much I love you!
> I'd sell off the whole world to get you back,
>   trade the creation just for you.
> So don't be afraid: I'm with you.
>
> (ISAIAH 43:1–5 MSG)

"That's from Isaiah," she squealed. "Isn't it great? Good-bye!"

She hung up on me. But she had left behind hope. God has not forgotten you, even when you're living where the sun don't shine. Even the people waiting to get on the plane could hear the tapping sound as that stake was driven firmly into the ground. How amazing that the scripture Chonda read contained almost the same message as Jadyn's prayer the night before.

I look back less now. It's difficult to look back while running full speed ahead. A lot of what I write is about *this* day, *this* moment. With whatever strength I have, I want my life to glorify the One who brought me through the valley and pointed me toward life fully alive. I'm stronger and more determined to live than ever before, setting goals I never dreamed possible. I just signed up for another triathlon, and I'm determined to run a marathon.

So many of the dreams I've seen fulfilled began as notes scrawled on tattered pages of a leather-covered notebook. Almost every worthy goal I've ever dared to commit to writing has become a reality. Keep a record! Watch the hand of God move in your life.

I can almost hear you murmuring, "I don't know where to start! I don't know how to do this." My advice to you is to grab a pencil and a notebook. Sit down and begin, "Dear Diarrhea," then just keep writing. If it works for a four-year-old, it can work for you.

Chapter Fifteen

WHAT'S LOVE GOT TO DO WITH IT?

NO MATTER HOW FRANTICALLY I SEARCH THE THESAURUS for the right words and try to arrange them on paper, I can't find a way to describe the depth of love I felt as I held Jadyn in the moments after her rescue. I didn't want to let her go. I find the same difficulty expressing the love I have for Diane, my children, and all my grandchildren. Those who are gifted enough to even come close to describing the power of love end up writing hit songs and beautiful poetry that instantly connects with the human heart. Friends can make the difference between success and failure in any venture you pursue. Without them life is almost unbearable. But without love there is nothing. In the 1960s, Jackie DeShannon sang, "What the world needs now is love, sweet love."[1] I wonder if the writers of that song or the millions who hummed the tune knew how incredibly "right on" those lyrics were.

In the year 2000, Rick and Patti White flew to the city of Vinnytsia, Ukraine. They had been planning the trip for three years, ever since their daughter Tori came home from a mission trip and announced that her heart had been stolen by a ten-year-old girl. Olena Morgan lived at the orphanage where Tori had volunteered. After only four hours with Olena, Tori fell in love and wanted to make her part of the family. When love makes an entrance, you can't ignore it. Now the Whites were in the Ukraine to move ahead with the adoption process.

As the time grew near, the Whites were encouraged to tell Olena of their plans. They had hesitated because they were afraid she would be disappointed if the adoption fell through. Olena was thrilled when she heard the news; her life suddenly filled with hope. Someone cared! Someone loved her! When they asked her if she wanted to be part of their family, she answered in two words: "Yes! When?"

The Whites returned to the United States to prepare for their new daughter. Tori made Olena a calendar with pictures of the house, family members, and pets that would soon be a part of her life, all designed to mark down the days left until they would all be together.

The Whites were making final plans to return to Vinnytsia, complete the legal process, and bring Olena home, when they got an overseas call urging them to "get over here right away." A Ukrainian nun was contesting the adoption, and there was a chance they might lose Olena forever! Patti caught the next flight for Ukraine. Unknown to her, while she was in the air, a hearing took place in a Vinnytsia courtroom. The judge asked Olena if she wanted to live with the nun. Olena's response was firm and without hesitation. "I already have a mother named Patti. She lives in the United States and is coming to get me." Because Olena was ten, the court had to abide by her wishes. Had the nun contested the adoption a few weeks earlier, before Olena's birthday, the girl would have had no say in the matter.

The day of the adoption, Rick and Patti stood in that same courtroom and heard words that pierced their hearts. A foreign adoption would be approved only because Olena had no family in Ukraine. Three times the judge made the same proclamation, repeating exactly the same words. Each time he began with, "Because you are unwanted and unloved by anyone in this nation . . ."

Rick flinched with every repetition of those cold, horrible words. By the third time, his eyes brimmed with tears. Olena stood resolute and didn't bat an eye. After the proclamation rang out for the final time, Rick squeezed Olena's tiny hand, leaned over to her, and said, "You will never, ever hear those words again. We love you and want you more than anything in the world."

With that, Olena became a member of the White family. That night they all went out for a celebration. Olena ordered salted herring and chased it down with ice cream. If you can survive that, you can survive anything.

After they all returned to the United States, Olena had the chance to pick her new English name. From several choices she chose Hope. Having met her and heard her story, I cannot imagine a more appropriate name. Today Hope is a senior in college, still a bundle of energy, spreading joy wherever she goes.

Someone came to Rick recently after hearing this story and said, "What a lucky little girl."

"You really have it backwards," Rick answered. "We're the ones who are blessed. I can't describe what joy her love has brought to our household. Watching her touch lives and seeing her giving spirit and determination will bless us forever." The Bible says three of the greatest things in life are faith, hope, and love. The White family is blessed with all three.

A BROADER PERSPECTIVE

"What the world needs now is love, sweet love" are lyrics that only brush the surface of the full dimension of love demonstrated by our Creator. His love is the foundation of hope, the essence of living fully alive. Depending on a person's health and physical condition, he can survive without food somewhere between forty and seventy days. Depending on the ambient temperature, a person can survive from two days to around thirty days without water. Without love we can survive for many years, but not fully alive. Life without love is merely existence. As I look back at the stakes in my life that became markers for living fully alive, I can see that they were placed in the ground by people who loved me, and that those stakes helped lead me to the wonderful life I enjoy today. I soak up love like a sponge.

Most wonderful of all is the strength and faith I found by trusting in the love demonstrated by Christ. I had known that love since early childhood, but the image and true depth of that love came into clearer focus as I saw it lived out in the lives of others. Being loved was like being filled with a tank of premium gas. It gave me the fuel to press on. It was my motivation and model to love others.

My first glimpse of unshakable love was the unconditional love of my wife. There were times in our marriage when Diane could have given up on me. Instead, she chose to love. When I was stumbling off the path of living fully alive, Diane knew God loved me, and she was willing to wait for Him to bring me back to my senses. In the midst of the valley of the shadow of death, she never left my side. I am forever grateful for her persistent love.

Having children allowed me to get an even broader perspective of God's love. If being loved is the premium gas that allows us to navigate the highways of life, loving others is the rocket fuel that makes life a thrilling, white-knuckle adventure.

I didn't want children. Not that I didn't like children; it's just that I had met one. That was as close as I wanted to get. For me children were kind of like monkeys: fun to watch scamper around, throw things, and have screeching fights with one another in the zoo, but I didn't want any piece of that action at home. Fairly early in our marriage Diane and I joined some friends for dinner at their house. I was seated next to a small, food-covered child who slobbered like a St. Bernard. Before the night was over, my wife and I had dodged plates and silverware, but we were soon covered with food ourselves. It was a long evening and a quiet ride home. Finally I spoke: "I don't want to have children."

I glanced over and saw Diane wiping food stains from her new dress. "Neither do I," she said.

I pulled onto the shoulder of the road, stopped the car, and took her hands in mine. "My love is reserved for you," I crooned. "I will share it with no child."

Then we went home and celebrated. Don't ever tell me God doesn't have a sense of humor. That very night our first daughter was conceived.

I remember when the doctor brought that baby to me for the first time. She wrapped four tiny little fingers around my pinky finger and wrapped her soul around my heart. In an instant I went from a reluctant father to a head-over-heels-in-love daddy. I looked into that tiny face and knew I would die for this child. I got a glimpse of how fierce, protective, and all-consuming God's love is. My love for this new life opened my eyes further to what living fully alive is all about. It's about love. It's about life focused on someone besides yourself. Children don't care about our title or how much money we make. They don't care if we are good-looking or have six-pack abdominals. They love us for who we are.

THE LOVE MONSTER

"What could be better?" I asked myself smugly, leaning back in a comfortable lounge chair on one of the country's most beautiful beaches.

Spread out before me was the Gulf of Mexico. Sitting beside me was opportunity personified: a producer who wanted me to appear in one of his films. No, it wasn't a big-budget, action thriller; it was an industrial training film. But that didn't matter. This was my big chance, my first step toward stardom on the silver screen. I scanned the gripping script of our blockbuster, oblivious to the fact that my daughter Taryn had slipped away from her mother and was wading in the hotel sewage pond. With a gorgeous beach at her disposal, Taryn preferred the little green pond with the big smell because, as she explained later, she liked the colors better.

As I dreamed of stardom, Taryn was festooning her little body with reeking algae. Then, completely cloaked in stringy goop, she came galloping toward me bathed in fumes rank enough to clear the entire beach. One instant I was reading a script; the next I looked up to see The Thing attacking at point-blank range. It hit me at fifteen miles an hour with enough impact to unwrap the clammy slime from around it and wrap it around me. I tried to get up, but the angle of the chair and the slipperiness of The Thing's arms around my neck pinned me in a tiny but effective hammerlock.

It grabbed me by the hair, pulled my head back, looked deep into my eyes, and proclaimed, "I love you! I love you! I love you! I kill you with love because I am The Love Monster!" It then proceeded to attack me mercilessly with sloppy, odorous kisses.

Appalled and disgusted, Mr. Movie Mogul leapt to his feet

and stiffly brushed bits of algae from his fancy shirt. "Could you please ask her to leave until our business is finished?" he sniffed.

Dripping with goop and still in the grip of The Love Monster, I responded, "Our business is finished now." I had no desire to do business with someone who could remain unmoved by the words of a child shouting, "I love you!" no matter how smelly or slime-covered.

It is because we are created in the image of God that we desire to love and be loved. One of the sources of my spiritual emptiness came from an innate sense of the disconnect I felt from the love of God at that time in my life. Living in a world where we are loved for what we can produce, how we look, what contribution we can make to society, leaves us with an insatiable desire to be loved instead for who we are. The essence of spiritual wholeness is a surrender that acknowledges God's love and returns that love to Him. As I look back at the stakes in my life, I see a distinct pattern where my life was shaped by understanding the importance of love and hearing the declaration of love.

I was speaking at Soldier Field for one of the early Promise Keepers events. The stadium and infield were packed with tens of thousands of men and their sons. The ages ranged from young dads with small boys to elderly fathers leaning on middle-aged sons. As fire hoses sprayed a fine mist over the hottest parts of the infield to bring relief from the oppressive heat, I challenged dads and sons to declare their love for one another. "Stand up, grab your son or your dad, bear-hug him, and tell him that you love him." You would've thought I'd asked these men to try on panty hose. Fifty thousand men and their offspring turned all squirrelly. They looked like fifth graders at a Sadie Hawkins dance. The meeting was being video recorded, and I had a monitor in front of me that displayed the image of a man and his son. The father looked like he might be a successful business-man, capable of leading a boardroom of power brokers, and the boy could have been a fearless linebacker on any football team. But here they were doing some kind of primitive dance around one another, unable or afraid to connect.

I grabbed the microphone. "Gentlemen," I said, "if we're unable to say the words 'I love you' to our own flesh and blood, we haven't got any message for the world. We might as well go home. Promise Keepers means nothing unless there is some kind of promise to keep. 'I love you' is God's promise. It's also His command that we love each other. Either we believe it as a family, or we don't believe it at all. All I'm asking is that you tell your sons and fathers that you love them."

A sacred rumble filled the stadium. I glanced down at the monitor again. The camera was still focused on the same man and his son, only now they unashamedly embraced each other, tears streaming down their faces.

That experience reminded me how important it is to love and be loved, and how critical it is to hear the words that con-firm it. Inside the heart of every man and woman is a wound that can only be healed by hearing those words and believing them.

A man waving his arms caught my eye as he stumbled up the center aisle from the far end of the stadium. Finally he stood at the base of the stage, out of breath, shouting at me. I put the microphone behind me and leaned forward, "Can I help you?"

"I've lost my father," he shouted.

I responded with genuine sympathy, "I'm so sorry."

"No," he protested, "I don't mean he's dead. I've lost him. He's somewhere here in the crowd." He gestured in the gen-eral direction of fifty thousand men. "I'm Bill Golden, and my father's name is Jim. I want to tell him I love him!" (I'll use ficti-tious names here because I don't remember the real ones.)

I put the microphone to my lips. "Gentlemen, I have a man down here named Bill Golden, and he has somehow misplaced his father, Jim. Jim, if you're out there, Bill wants you to meet him at the front of the stage so he can tell you he loves you."

Suddenly the aisles were filled with other men and boys who had also been separated from each other, now inspired to reconnect. Men were willing to run the length of a football stadium for the chance to hear the life-giving sound of the words *I love you*. Bill's words echo in my head even to this day: "I've lost my father." I wonder how many men and women go to bed every night with an aching heart. People who feel that living fully alive is out of reach because they've found nothing to heal the wounds in their hearts. Little do they know it's because they've lost touch with "the Father"—the only One who can heal the wounded heart.

I love you. Those three words are absolutely essential to being fully alive. They are words we were born to hear. There is no substitute for them; nothing can take their place. I know this because there was a time when I longed to hear those words and did not.

When I was a child, it was considered less than masculine for a man to express his feelings of love. Superheroes like John Wayne, the Lone Ranger, and Mighty Mouse were willing to go to great lengths to save lives but never declared their love with the three magic words. Romantic leading men could bestow breathtaking kisses and rib-crushing embraces, they could whisk a woman across the threshold to a bedroom, but rarely did you hear a man say the words *I love you*. I'm not ashamed to admit that I say those words to my grandchildren and children and wife almost every time I see them. I even declare my love to my sons-in-law (even though they don't deserve it). Seriously, I need to hear those words. Whether you sit in a corporate tower or dig a ditch, whether you live in a gated community or a trailer park, no matter what your sex or station in life, at the very core of your being is a need to be loved.

BETWEEN THE LINES

After receiving a Gold Medallion Book Award for my book *Jumper Fables*, I sped to the airport to catch a flight home. Tucked under my arm was a plaque engraved with my name, commemorating the honor. When the plane leveled off at thirty-five thousand feet, I tipped my seat back to catch up on some sleep and glanced up at the overhead bin where the plaque was stored.

Without warning I started sobbing. Not the quiet, respectable sobs of an adult but the choking, uncontrollable, snot-yielding sobs of a child. Tears streamed down my cheeks. The man sitting next to me handed me the little tablecloth from the back of his tray. I used all of it. Some deep emotion that had been hiding for years in a subterranean level of my soul evidently decided to come up for air. Now that it was exposed to light, it became apparent that this was not a wispy aspiration. It was full-grown, HD-quality, focused, and ugly.

Suddenly I recognized the monster. I realized what it was that had wandered down there silent and unresolved for so many years. It was the desire to hear my dad say, "I love you." I wanted my dad to see my Gold Medallion plaque. I wanted to hear him say, "I'm proud of you." Even now it's a little hard to admit this, but I know I'm not alone. I have met burly men behind prison bars and sat with professional football players who expressed the same intense emotion I felt that day. In fact, it was the search for love in all the wrong places that led many of those men to the desperate deeds that destroyed their lives.

My dad's generation expressed love by putting food on the table and a roof over our heads, and for that faithful expression of love I am grateful. But real men didn't outwardly express love or sorrow with spoken words. That was a sign of vulnerability. My dad was a superhero. He had survived three and a half years as a prisoner of war where being vulnerable led to death. It was almost impossible for him to open up and confess his feelings for another grown person. I don't think I ever doubted my dad's love for me, but there, at thirty-five thousand feet, surrounded by strangers, I suddenly had a desperate longing to hear him speak the words that would confirm it.

I pulled a piece of paper from my briefcase and wrote the first and only letter I ever wrote specifically to my father. I poured out my heart, telling him about the award I had received. I confessed that much of my driven personality came from my desire to please him and make him proud of me. I expressed my deep love for him and, with a trembling hand, wrote of how I wanted to hear him say "I love you."

I can still see the mailbox and smell the freshly mown grass of that morning when I mailed the letter. I can hear the metallic sound the little red flag made as I tipped it up so the postman would be sure to take this special delivery. For days afterward, whenever the phone rang, I would leap to answer it. It might be Dad! He had read my letter, and now I would hear the words I was born to hear.

Days became weeks and weeks stretched into months. Anticipation was replaced by disappointment. Disappointment degenerated into anger. An ominous ghost of doubt skulked nearby, begging to be embraced. "Maybe he doesn't love you," the ghost smirked. "Maybe you have to do more, achieve more, or be better to gain his respect and love. The award for your book wasn't enough. Even your letter wasn't enough."

Those emotions still simmered as my wife and I drove from Colorado to northern Minnesota to visit my parents. As we pulled into the driveway after twelve hours of butt-numbing travel, anger boiled to the surface and summoned the ghost. I could feel it probing for access to my heart. Why hadn't Dad at least acknowledged getting the letter? Did he even get it? What will I say when I see him?

I walked in without knocking and was immediately greeted by my startled and surprised mom. Mom surprises easily; she would have been surprised even if I had called her from the porch and told her we were about to open the door. Dad came and gave each of us his trademark manly wrestler hug. I'm sure I was stiff and unresponsive, but he didn't seem to notice. After the initial greetings he disappeared into the garage where old lawnmowers, oily chainsaws, and beat-up snowmobiles stood in testimony to his master skill of fixing the unfixable.

Immediately my mom pulled me aside. "I want to show you something," she said, motioning for me to follow. She led me into their bedroom. The room was lit only by a small lamp on a table against the wall. Sitting near the lamp was my college graduation picture. The wall above the table was covered with dozens of newspaper clippings—interviews and reviews of my shows sent to my dad by friends and relatives. I recognized some that I had enclosed in letters home. Nestled among the clippings was an article with a picture of me receiving the Gold Medallion Book Award for *Jumper Fables*.

Then a small framed picture caught my eye. "Your dad made that frame," Mom said as I moved closer in the dim light. It wasn't a picture. Dad had framed the letter I'd written at thirty-five thousand feet. My knees buckled as I reached for a place to sit on the end of the bed. Tears and sobs and snot again made their dramatic entrance.

"Stop sending your father stuff," Mom said with a flair of mock annoyance. "He's turning our bedroom into a shrine." Indeed, for me it was a shrine. That dimly lit wall screamed to me the words my dad couldn't say: "I love you, son. You are my pride and joy." With an audible groan the ghost of doubt disappeared—never to be seen again.

I've scavenged my brain to remember if there was a time my dad ever verbally said "I love you," unfettered by qualifiers such as "I love you, but it's with godly love." I don't mean to diminish God's love, but I needed to hear my dad say *he* loved me with *his* love. If he ever said it, that memory is lost somewhere. I can't find it. Life had not taught my dad the verbal language of love. I think he wanted to say it; he just didn't know how. But he sure knew how to write it on a wall.

I'm confident he knows how to say it now. He was buried with honors in Fort Snelling National Cemetery. But he is not there. He is with the One who said, "I love you best of all." Ken Davis Sr. was set free forever on April 18, 2006. He lives now with the Lord he loved so much. When I see him again, I know the first words I will hear . . . unless I beat him to it.

At my father's memorial service I made two resolutions.

First, I resolved to confirm my love to people I care for—with words. My family, my friends, and my Savior long to hear "I love you." I have resolved to say it often, out loud.

Second, I resolved to strive to see the unspoken proclamations of "I love you." I would look for it between the lines in the note from my child. I would hear the words when Diane squeezed my hand. In the sunrise and in the sudden downpour of rain, I would listen to God saying, "I love you."

Stop. Take a deep breath. Realize that you are alive and have the hope of eternal life. Do you hear it? Read between those lines. Do you see it? You are *loved.*

SAY IT OUT LOUD

I challenge young people around the world to deliberately express love to their families. At the risk of sounding like a total emotional pushover, I will tell you one more story to show you why. When my daughter Traci was thirteen, she stopped saying "I love you." No matter what I did, I couldn't get her to say it. I would look at her and say, "I love you," then pause and nod my head in a way that indicated very clearly, "Now it's your turn to say those words." She would say, "Me too." Then I would say, "Well, then say it." And she would say, "I just did." "Me too" is not the same as "I love you."

After her sixteenth birthday party, we were cleaning up in the kitchen. I took my daughter by the shoulders, turned her around, looked her in the eye, and I said, "I love you."

"Whatever," she replied, then turned around and went back to doing her dishes.

To any teenager who might have been forced to read this book, I implore you: don't stop saying "I love you" to your parents. I know that our culture doesn't consider it cool for teenagers to openly express love toward their parents, but neither did my dad's culture. Forget the culture because the culture is wrong. Jesus said, "As I have loved you, so you must love one another" (John 13:34). He expressed His love in the most profound way: "Greater love has no one than this, that he lay down his life for his friends" (John 15:13). But Jesus also made sure He left a written record that would serve as His verbal declaration. The basic, bottom-line message of the Bible, all the way from Genesis to the maps, is this: the Creator of the universe saying to you and me, "I love you," and then proving it with His life. Even as an adult I read the account of His love over and over. It sustains me. It fires me, motivates me to live with adventure and excellence. If we intend to live fully alive, the chain of silence has to be broken. Say the words.

I was crushed by my daughter's response but chalked it up to the fact that I'm a wimp. So I covered up my disappointment. Two years passed, and the time came for me to take Traci to college. I flew her to John Brown University and dropped her off in a tiny room with all her possessions in a cardboard box. As I stood in that room, I realized that the curtains had closed on one chapter of her life, and another chapter had begun. Things would never be the same. I would not have the same leading role I'd had ever since she was born. Now I would have a supporting role. My part would be limited to walk-on bits and cameo appearances. Before I left that little dorm room, I said it one more time: "I love you." She answered, "Me too," and began to unpack.

It was a very difficult flight home. In spite of all I had achieved, regardless of the fact that I was flying my own private airplane or that people around the world wanted to hear me speak, I just wanted to hear "I love you" from an eighteen-year-old girl.

One year later the chaplain at John Brown University invited me to speak at a chapel service. I returned to that campus filled with fear and anxiety. I love standing in front of a crowd. I love applause now as much as I did when I was prancing in front of the radio in my saggy diaper. There is no place I am more comfortable than on a stage. But this time my daughter would be in the audience, and I was terrified. When the service was over, the chaplain took me to lunch at a nice Italian restaurant with bright red-and-white-checkered tablecloths and the smell of garlic almost visible in the air.

As we began to eat, the chaplain opened his briefcase. "I thought you would like to see these," he said, showing me the case overflowing with three-by-five cards. "These are student-response cards from the chapel service. Sometimes we get half a dozen, sometimes we'll get a couple hundred, but this is overwhelming. Let me read you some of them."

He grabbed a handful and began to read. "This is the best speaker we've ever had." "The combination of inspiration and humor was amazing." "This guy rocks." It was very gratifying to hear the positive feedback. Then he reached into his pocket and pulled out a single card. "Here's one I thought might interest you," he said, handing it to me as I took a large mouthful of spaghetti. On the front of the card was my daughter's name, Traci Lynn Davis. I froze. I was afraid to turn it over and read her comment. What would she say? Finally I flipped it over, and on the other side in big, round letters, she had written, "I love my daddy."

I spit spaghetti all over the table. I excused myself and ran for the bathroom, slamming the big green door shut behind me, then locking it with one of those old bolt locks where you push the little knob up and slide the latch shut. I just stood inside that bathroom and wailed: "She loves me! She loves me! She does love me!"

Suddenly I heard a voice from the stall say, "Get a life, man!" I jumped about two feet in the air. I had assumed I was the only one in the room. It was one of the few times in my life when I didn't appreciate having an audience.

As I made a hasty retreat, I knew from the depths of my soul that without love there is no life. You can be in perfect physical shape, you can be the most famous person on the planet, you can have every material possession you dreamed of, but without love there is nothing.

HEALING THE WOUNDED HEART

During those years I leaned heavily on my family to heal the wound in my own heart. As I look back, I can see that was a mistake. There are very few things more harmful than to expect from another human being what only God can supply. As I began to breathe and move and live, I started to trust God to heal that wound, risking my soul by believing and behaving as though He loved me more than I loved my family. In the process of learning that His love was solid and unshakable and that there were no strings attached, my wound began to heal. When God treats the wound in a heart, it doesn't heal without a scar. The balm that He uses fills the gaping hole and then overflows, empowering us to love other people with the same kind of love and giving us the opportunity to help heal the hearts of others. His love is the perfect example of "what the world needs now."

Just before He was to be executed, Jesus gathered His disciples together and said this: "A new command I give you: Love one another. As I have loved you, so you must love one another. By this all men will know that you are my disciples, if you love one another" (John 13:34–35). The number one identifying factor of a true follower of Christ is love.

If I speak in the tongues of men and of angels, but have not love, I am only a resounding gong or a clanging cymbal. If I have the gift of prophecy and can fathom all mysteries and all knowledge, and if I have a faith that can move mountains, but have not love, I am nothing. If I give all I possess to the poor and surrender my body to the flames, but have not love, I gain nothing.

Love is patient, love is kind. It does not envy, it does not boast, it is not proud. It is not rude, it is not self-seeking, it is not easily angered, it keeps no record of wrongs. Love does not delight in evil but rejoices with the truth. It always protects, always trusts, always hopes, always perseveres.

Love never fails. But where there are prophecies, they will cease; where there are tongues, they will be stilled; where

there is knowledge, it will pass away. For we know in part and
we prophesy in part, but when perfection comes, the imperfect disappears. When I was a child, I talked like a child, I
thought like a child, I reasoned like a child. When I became
a man, I put childish ways behind me. Now we see but a poor
reflection as in a mirror; then we shall see face to face. Now
I know in part; then I shall know fully, even as I am fully
known.

And now these three remain: faith, hope and love. But
the greatest of these is love. (1 Corinthians 13)

There it is. It's impossible to truly love until you have experienced God's love. I wish I had caught that earlier in life. But I'm
so grateful to have caught it now.

The love of God our Father is the only love that eventually
can heal the wounds in our hearts. The best example of that love
is seen in the fierce love Jesus demonstrated on the cross. The
best glimpse we will get of that love on this earth is the love we
express toward each other. You want to live fully alive? In the
words of an old song, "You gotta love somebody." And that love
will be most fully expressed when we embrace the love of God
and are empowered to love beyond ourselves.

Beyond friendship, beyond physical health, life itself depends
on being loved and giving love. Those who do not know this
vital connection do not know life. They are hollow shells of existence waiting to experience the real essence of living fully alive.

Chapter Sixteen

SKATING WELL ON GOLDEN POND

DAVE VEERMAN, A VICE PRESIDENT WITH THE LIVINGSTONE
Group in Chicago, once lived in Covington, Louisiana. He'd
been training for a marathon run across the world's longest
bridge over water, a twenty-four-mile structure spanning Lake
Pontchartrain. Dave thought he was in good shape, but on the
day of the race a strong wind blowing directly in the face of
the runners put his endurance to the test. Fifteen miles into the
marathon, Dave was exhausted. Every part of his body hurt. His
will to continue was eroding. To make matters worse, women
pushing baby carriages were passing him like he was standing
still. He felt as if he'd had a blowout in both running shoes, but
he stumbled on. Every step was a major effort.

Dave lost track of time and distance until finally he began
to hear the cheers of the crowd at the finish line. He knew he was
close. Then he saw his family on the sidelines and the camcorder
in his wife's hands. "Suddenly," Dave said, "I felt that rush of

adrenaline. I couldn't let my family see me finish weakly. With only about a hundred yards to go, I straightened up, shrugged off my exhaustion, and sprinted the rest of the way to the finish line."

After Dave had rested, he and his family sat down at home to watch the video. Dave watched himself stagger into view like a dying man dragging himself across the desert. He saw the exact moment that the glint shone in his eyes as he realized he was being filmed. Then he saw himself take a deep breath and continue on with the same shuffling gait. He said he looked like an old man on his way to the bathroom in a pair of loose slippers. Although Dave had thought he was sprinting to the finish line, nothing had actually changed. Only his spirit was different. I laughed until I was sick when Dave told me that story.

But as a man at a stage in life where I can see the finish line from here, I see differently than I did years ago. Today I would shake Dave's hand and congratulate him. He did not finish weakly; he finished well. Helicopters covering the race had captured images of dozens who had given up. Some of the runners who had sprinted to the front early in the race now sat by the edge of the road, waiting for a ride. When I ran my triathlon, my goal was to finish well. When people gather to celebrate my life, I want them to say I finished well.

Let the slim mothers pushing baby carriages pass if they wish. I will run at my pace fully alive. Even if I shuffle, crawl, or have friends carry me across, I will refuse to give up until I make it to the finish line. I don't want to sit on the sidelines. I don't want to lose sight of the goal that has driven my life since my first memories. I've asked my friends to hold me to my promise that I will keep running until I break the tape that separates this world from the next. One of those friends gave me a coin I carry with me. The coin is imprinted with the words *Be encouraged. Finish well.*

The beautiful 1981 film *On Golden Pond*, starring Henry Fonda and Katharine Hepburn, followed an older, deeply-in-love couple as they spent what could have been one of their final summers on Golden Pond. I enjoyed the movie, but even back then I wished there had been more life in it. All the hugging and kissing and conversation was great, but I wanted to see a water fight. I wanted to see Henry throw Katharine off the end of the dock. Or maybe a canoe race or a rock-skipping contest, something that showed that these people were still in gear. I know. I know. Their love sustained them. I value that. But oh, how I wish the last scene had been filmed right after the pond froze over. I can see the sunset as it cast its red glow onto the ice. How I would have loved to see those two skating as fast as they could, clumsily holding hands, barely keeping their balance as the sound of their laughter echoed across the ice. I wanted to see them fall and slide spinning across the frozen surface with squeals of delight, then fade to black.

As you skate onto Golden Pond, don't do it timidly.

Laugh whenever you can.

Throw someone off the dock.

Find a cause bigger than yourself.

Pray for the impossible.

Dust off that Schwinn.

Get to know someone with a piercing.

Spread the good news of God's love with boldness.

Don't show anyone your scars.

Nap, but not while driving.

Stay curious.

Take a college course.

Learn something new.

Live.

Robert Wickman has been quoted as having said, "Life is not a journey to the grave with the intention of arriving safely in a pretty and well-preserved body, but rather to skid in broadside, thoroughly used up, totally worn out, and loudly proclaiming, 'Wow . . . what a ride!'"

Before we strap on the skates, I want to want to talk to you fortunate younger people who don't even think about growing older. Listen! Finishing well is not a topic just for old people. Skating well on Golden Pond starts now. The decisions you make today will determine whether someday you just fade into the sunset or slide in headfirst shouting, "Wow . . . what a ride!"

DRIPS

I was amazed when I recently saw my old friend Phil Waldrep. He looked twenty years younger, and there was vitality in his step that hadn't been there before. After years of being overweight, Phil had decided to take action. He started walking regularly, limited his calorie intake to match his lifestyle, and lost sixty pounds. Phil said that losing weight was the most expensive decision he ever made. He had to buy a whole new wardrobe. He had been wearing the same old rags for years and now was learning to shop all over again. What a great problem! Phil said he was faced with a dilemma. "Should I throw the old clothes away, or should I keep them, you know, in case I gain weight back again?" Throwing away old clothes that are too big is not wasteful; it's a good way to keep from being waist-full.

"Are you kidding?" I answered. "That's like an alcoholic saving a jug of whiskey in case he decides to drink again."

Not everybody will cheer your efforts to be healthier. Phil says that people who haven't seen him for a while don't know what to say when they see his new physique. Some ask him if he's been sick. One lady, after checking to be sure no one was listening, walked up to him and said, "I know how you feel."

Phil was puzzled. "What do you mean?" he asked.

She leaned forward and whispered, "Cancer. I've had it too."

In a country where one out of every three adults and one out of every six children is certifiably obese, we look at people who lose weight as abnormal. Something must be wrong. I have known Phil for a long time and know he cares far less about how he looks than he does about his newly found ability to live fully alive. Phil will probably never run a marathon or swim in the lane next to me in a triathlon. But he walks almost every day, and he eats right. He continues to do the math. He inspires me. Young energetic friends, here's why you have an advantage. You have time now to build what you will become . . . one drip at a time.

Phil told me this story: Something was wrong with his home. Walls were cracking, and doors wouldn't shut. After a careful inspection a contractor led my friend to one corner of his house where the rainspout had been dripping for years. Removing the dirt at that corner of the house revealed that the entire foundation in that spot had suffered severe erosion. That end of the house was literally falling down. The culprit wasn't a sudden torrent of water but one tiny, neglected drip of water that over a period of years was ruining an entire home.

Foundations are built strong or destroyed one drip at a time. As a young boy I visited Carlsbad Caverns in New Mexico. I remember standing in a big room, looking at a stalagmite the size of a building. The guide told us that this beautiful structure was the result of mineral-rich water dripping one drip at a time over a period of thousands of years. The structures that built from the floor up were called stalagmites because, according to the guide, they *might* reach the ceiling. The monstrous icicle-like formations that hung from above were called stalactites because they held *tight* to the ceiling. Individual drips of water are capable of building spectacular beauty or causing untold destruction. Perhaps one of the reasons the stalactites and stalagmites resulted in such beauty is that they were both anchored to something.

So before you start to shuffle and wrinkle, take this bit of wisdom from someone who has been there. There is no such thing as a small choice. The choices you make today affect your tomorrow. Those tiny little choices become habits that eventually destroy the foundations of your life or lead you toward living fully alive. Beauty or destruction. Either way, it's your choice.

MAKE YOUR BED

Every Tuesday night a group of friends from Franklin, Tennessee, get together for dinner and a night of laughter and camaraderie that I rarely miss. One of the regulars is a delightfully feisty young woman about my age. Her name is Patsy Clairmont, and, yes, we're old enough to have our skates on and tightly laced. As a young bride Patsy began to experience severe panic attacks. She would be sitting in church and suddenly, for no apparent reason, her heart would start to race. Patsy says it was terrifying, like the world was about to come to an end. These attacks were so devastating she would be rushed to the hospital by her husband, and fear of the attacks would cause Patsy never to go back to that church again. Patsy had attacks in grocery stores, driving down the road, and visiting friends. Each time she would retreat into an ever-shrinking world. Eventually, even her own home terrified her, and finally the only place she felt safe was in her bed. She begged God to show her how to escape this prison of fear.

When you lie in bed day after day, there's nowhere else to run. Patsy said that one day, deep in her spirit, she heard a voice, almost as if God where speaking audibly. She believes it was God answering her prayer. The voice said, "Make your bed." Now that doesn't sound like a very dramatic intervention. What kind of difference could that possibly make in a life that seemed destined to hopeless despair? Nonetheless, Patsy got up and made her bed. Shortly after that she was compelled to vacuum the floor. Step by step she reentered the land of the living.

Today Patsy Clairmont travels across America, touring with Women of Faith. Her inspirational story has changed the lives of thousands of women and had an impact on more than a few men, myself included. If there is an ice skating race on Golden Pond, I don't want to compete against Patsy. She's not finishing well because she's preparing to die. She's finishing well because she has insisted on living. None of us would ever have been blessed by this vivacious woman of faith if she hadn't listened as a young woman to the Spirit of God urging her to make her bed. So don't skip the rest of this chapter because you're young. This chapter will help you stay young.

I don't remember when I first realized I was growing older. It might have been the day I looked in the mirror and saw my dad. I turned around to see if he was standing behind me. I certainly realized I was getting "up there" when a lovely, elderly woman grabbed my hand and with stars in her eyes said, "I heard you speak when I was in high school." There's a terrible temptation for my generation to shift into neutral. After all, what good is it to dream about castles if I don't have enough time to build them? Why try to stay fit when each year my body is able to do less than it did the year before?

I wasted one whole day thinking about retirement. I imagined a life with no more security pat downs, delayed flights, or book deadlines. What would it be like to fill my days playing golf and watching game shows on television? I knew the answer before I finished the question. Boring! It didn't take long to eliminate retirement as a possibility. It was my body that first whispered, "You are no longer the man you once were." It was the challenge to live fully alive that drove me to be *better* than the man I once was. I'm embracing this season of life. I'm not going to retire. I'm going to retread and keep right on going. I feel like my age is an advantage.

Younger people have to ponder decisions without the benefit of experience. Which way do I turn? Will this work? What is the first step? If you've been there and done that, then you can move forward more quickly, with confidence. I don't have to rely on trial and error; I've already tried and erred so many times I know right where to go to get 'er done. I might just build that castle; it certainly would take less time. Sometimes I dream of what it would be like to be young again. To sleep the entire night without having to visit what my uncle tactfully called Mr. Rogers' neighborhood. I'm suspicious that in order to regain a youthful body I would have to give up the wisdom from these years of experience. No, thank you. I'll put up with a few aches and pains and hang on to the brains. When my brain goes, perhaps then I'll be ready to plea-bargain for a complete makeover. Then I remember I'm already scheduled for a complete makeover. When I break that tape at the finish line, everything will be new again. Until then, I intend to live! My grandchildren want me to live and run and play. A few years ago they begged me to build a tree house. I remember thinking, *I can't build a tree house. I can't even get up in a tree.* Then I met Fanny.

FANNY

Across the road and down the hollow from our home in Tennessee lives a wonderful woman we affectionately call Fanny. It's impossible to tell how old she is by simply looking at her. She lives alone out here in the country, gets around better than a lot of younger folks I know, and has refused to retire from life. When Fanny's husband died, instead of allowing her life to shrink into a few rooms and a stack of old scrapbooks, she continued to live. This was not a woman who would drift off slowly into the sunset.

One set of neighbors tells of meeting Fanny. They had heard there was an older woman living down the road, so they stopped to assure her they would check on her once in a while. After meeting her, the neighbors decided it would be better to have Fanny check on them.

We discovered that Fanny built her own house. She found an old abandoned building, did research to find the owner, and bought the house with its foundation of hand-hewn boulders for five hundred dollars. Then she disassembled the building and moved it board by board and stone by stone to her property in the hollow. All but the biggest stones and beams she hauled in her station wagon. She hired out work that required heavy machinery, had a contractor pour the cement, and got help with the beams she couldn't lift by herself. Basically, Fanny built her own house with her own hands. If there's some kind of disaster or flood or snowstorm, I'm counting on Fanny to come check on me.

Her home is beautiful. When my granddaughters visit, they always want to go see Miss Fanny. Fanny is tall and slim and moves with the dignified elegance of an aristocrat. When she talks, her words are accompanied by expansive, graceful gestures. And her face. Oh, how I love her face. When she talks to my granddaughters, they cannot take their eyes from Fanny's. "Oh, you are the most beautiful girls I've ever laid eyes on," she declares in her genteel Southern accent, every line in that wonderful face punctuating her adoration for my girls.

When she speaks of things that disturb her, those same lines rearrange themselves to leave no doubt concerning her displeasure. A visitor never needs to guess how Fanny feels about an issue. Some people wear their hearts on their sleeves. Fanny's heart can be seen in her beautifully expressive face. Everything about Fanny radiates the joy of the moment. "You sit right there, and I'm going to get you some tea," she tells my granddaughters. "Oh, you're perfect! You are!" And then she will go get tea for them. If there's anything my granddaughters like more than tea with Fanny, I have yet to see it.

Out back the girls and I sit in a porch swing that looks like it was made out of some kind of ingenious woven leather straps. One day I asked her where she got such a beautiful and expertly crafted swing.

"I made it," she explained, as though people normally make their own swings. She wasn't bragging. I don't think Fanny would brag if you held hot coals to her feet. "That's hickory bark. I cut down a hickory tree over there," she said, setting down her teacup to point farther down the hollow. "I stripped off the outer bark so I could get to the under-bark. It's pliable like leather. Of course, this can only be done in the springtime." I nodded as if I already knew this can only be done in the springtime. The grandchildren sipped tea and listened with wide eyes. "Once the outer layer was off, I shaved that wonderful second layer into uniform strips and wove it into the design on this swing."

"And what about these?" I asked, pointing at the unique arrangement of rings that holds the swing to the ceiling of the porch. "Those are from old mule harnesses," she laughed. "I had to search everywhere for them and finally found a hardware store that had a bucketful." Only the sound of the creaking swing and children slurping tea filled a break in the conversation.

"I just love to sit out here and enjoy the breeze." Fanny paused for a moment as she watched the little girls trying their best to be dainty, holding their teacups with two fingers, their pinkies extended. She smiled at me and added nonchalantly, "Sometimes I shoot rattlesnakes from up here." I love talking to people who are fully alive.

Fanny is a fixture in Franklin, Tennessee. She knows judges and landowners, shopkeepers and neighbors. She knows the history of our little town, and her family has played a part in that history. She is always helping those less fortunate than herself, and Fanny knows how to get things done. In her words, "You just do it!" If there's something Fanny needs to know, she will do the research to find it out. There's very little Fanny doesn't know.

The other day when I stopped to see her, she pointed out other projects she wanted to complete but couldn't because her gentleman friends were taking up too much of her time. I could write a whole book about Fanny, but nobody would believe it. I love Fanny. She is the antithesis of people who die at twenty-five but aren't buried until they're seventy-five. She's blown right past seventy-five with no signs of quitting. Advancing age, widowhood, helping a needy neighbor—Fanny takes them all in stride. And along the way she builds houses, rescues her neighbors, serves tea to little girls, and shoots rattlesnakes when the need arises.

Fanny visited with us yesterday. She told me she is almost eighty-six years old. The weatherman said it might snow hard tomorrow. I hope she checks on me. I want to show her the tree house I built. Remember that tree house? I did get it built. I got into the tree with a very long ladder and hundreds of short prayers.

SEE YOU AT THE HOUSE

God wants you to live. No matter what your age, He's not done with you yet. I've tasted the adventure that comes with living fully alive, and no matter what my circumstances, I want to continue to experience Christ and the power of His resurrection until I look Him in the face. Instead of retiring, I'm going to retread. That way I can get another hundred thousand miles out of this body. I may not do the same things I'm doing now, but my purpose will remain the same. I can continue to know Christ and experience the power of His resurrection whether I'm standing on a stage or lying in a hospital bed.

I sat in the second service of the People's Church in Franklin, Tennessee, one morning as Pastor Rick asked for prayer concerning a phone call he had received. An old friend named Wayne Allen had called him unexpectedly. Over the past few years they had lost touch with one another. Rick was delighted to hear the familiar voice ask, "What are you doing?" Rick filled him in on what was going on in his life and in the church.

Then Rick asked Wayne the same question: "How are you doing?" Wayne responded, "I am dying." The tone of his voice was unmistakable. This was not a joke. Over the past several years this big, robust man had fought valiantly as his heart began to fail. He had endured bypass procedures and a surgery to install a pacemaker, and now the doctors had told him they could do no more. He had only days, maybe hours, to live. Wayne was contacting friends he had not talked to for a while. Rick told Wayne he would come to Memphis to see him on Monday.

Rick asked us to pray that he would have an opportunity to say good-bye to his friend. I offered to fly Rick to Memphis in my plane. On the way he told me that Wayne Allen was what people call a prince of a man: a man of impeccable character who held tight to strong, conservative doctrine but never bashed or belittled those who disagreed with him. By the time we landed in Memphis, I felt like I knew Wayne myself. We rented a car and drove to his home, where we were greeted by his children, who had flown home from the mission field to be with their father in his last hours. Wayne was seated in an overstuffed chair beside his bed. Next to the chair sat a large green tank that helped his body get the oxygen his heart could no longer supply.

Rick and Wayne laughed and reminisced and talked for about an hour before Rick saw Wayne begin to tire. We gathered with the family around the big chair to pray with this sweet man. Then it was time to leave. This would be the last time Rick would see his friend. As he prepared to say good-bye, Rick debated with himself what to do. *What do I say?* he wondered silently. *Do I try to give words of hope? Do I say good-bye?* It was an emotional moment for everyone. Rick verbalized his struggle as we stood to leave. "I don't know what to say," he began. "I know this is what it is but . . ."

Wayne interrupted him. "Hey, Rick!" We saw the sweet glimmer of hope shining through those tired eyes as his face wrinkled in a smile. "I'll see you at the house!"

And we had worried about blessing him! We could have flown home without the plane. This was a man who was finishing well. Confined to a small bed and an overstuffed chair, unable to go anywhere without a big green tank, and with only days to live, he leaned into the tape, a photo finish of faith.

When I first started speaking about the subject of living fully alive, I entitled my talk "Live Until You Die." It wasn't until I experienced a renewal in my own spiritual life that I realized this was the wrong title. I changed the title to "Live Until You Live Forever." After I ran across St. Irenaeus's quote—"God's glory is the earth creature made fully and eternally alive"—I shortened the title to "Fully Alive." It covers everything. The so-called golden years are the best years of life. Many people in their golden age no longer have to make a living, so they are freer than ever to live. If your goal in life has been to retire, then what's to live for once you've done that? If your goal in life has been to glorify God by living fully alive, this season may be your best chance. Now you have time to do it.

YOU'RE NOT HOME YET

After fifty years of service in Africa, a weary missionary couple descended the gangplank of their boat. Their disembarking was delayed by a throng of press and well-wishers welcoming President Theodore Roosevelt back from his most recent safari. As they made their way through the crowd, the husband expressed to his wife how discouraged he was. After fifty years of spreading the gospel, after losing two children to jungle diseases, there was not a single person to welcome them home. His wife suggested that he talk to God about this during his bedtime prayers. In their cheap little hotel room the exhausted wife fell asleep almost immediately. She awoke in the morning to find her husband smiling and whistling softly as he prepared for the day.

"Boy," she said, "you have certainly lightened up. Did you tell God about your disappointment?"

"Yes, I did," he answered. "I told Him how sad and angry it made me that after all the years of service and sacrifice, we had no one to welcome us home."

"Well," his wife asked, "what did God say to you?"

With a smile her husband answered. "God said, 'You're not home yet.'"

What a jolt of encouragement! What a kick in the backside! What motivation for me to stop moaning and live life with gusto! In the midst of the worst of tribulations, the writer of Revelation encourages us to "be faithful, even to the point of death, and I will give you the crown of life" (Rev. 2:10). The best part is yet to come.

Chapter Seventeen

WHAT IF?

THE DAY JADYN WAS RESCUED IN THE MOUNTAINS IS etched permanently in my heart for two reasons. First, that day my priorities snapped into crystal-clear focus. I realized that all the trinkets and possessions in the universe take second place to relationships. That afternoon I would have traded everything I owned for the privilege of holding that little girl in my arms again. But something else happened that would etch the experience even deeper on the wall of my heart. When the celebration of Jadyn's rescue ebbed, an unanswered question began to rattle around in my brain like a marble in the bottom of an empty pail. I would hear the relentless rattle of that question constantly for the next year. As I stood in front of an audience telling the story of Jadyn's rescue, I could hear the marble. When I challenged people to trust Jesus and live fully alive, I could hear the marble. When I shouted the words, "God is good," the sound of the marble incessantly remained.

That marble was a question, and the question was simple: What if? I lay awake at night asking myself, "What if Jadyn had not been rescued? What if she had perished in the mountains? Would I still be able to stand in front of thousands of men and women and encourage them to trust a God who would allow a child to perish?"

I was numb to the fact that tens of thousands of children starve to death and thousands of innocent people die from disease and accidents every day. Tragedy is a constant in our world. The what-if question is pushed to a far corner of our brains until we are personally affected. When it's our child or our loved one who has been lost, then the marble is released and the what-if question is catapulted front and center.

For me, it wasn't as much a crisis of faith as it was a re-examination of my faith; but I knew that until I settled the issue, that marble would continue to roll and grow in volume. Eventually the sound would affect my ability to live fully alive.

A year after Jadyn's rescue, I returned to hunt elk in the area where she'd been lost. I was driving an all-terrain vehicle on the same old mining road we had taken to our campsite a year before. I rounded a curve and a flash of pink caught my eye. There at the side of the road, blowing gently in the breeze, was a length of pink ribbon tied to a bush. I choked back a sob as I realized it was the ribbon the rescue team had used a year before to mark the last spot Jadyn had been seen. Now it was a gentle reminder of the grace of God.

As I sat silently watching the ribbon flutter in the wind, the marble rolled to a stop. The incessant noise of the what-if question was gone, replaced with a hallowed silence that confirmed a truth I'd known all along. If there were ever a time I would need a faith that could sustain me, it would be in the what-if moment. If there were ever a time I would need assurance that there was a God who loved my little princess more than I did, it would be in the what-if moment. If there were ever a time I would need the hope of eternal life, it would be in the what-if moment.

Tears flowed freely as I sat in the silence of the wilderness. I got off the ATV and knelt at this unique altar. There I recommitted to spend the rest of my life sharing the hope of Christ and challenging men and women to live fully alive. I understand now why people of faith in the Bible built altars to remind themselves and generations to come of the goodness of God. I carefully untied the ribbon and took it home. Today it has a place of honor in my home as a memorial to the goodness of God. A God that is good not just in the good times but also in the what-if times of life. In abundant times and in the valleys of life, "we know that in all things God works for the good of those who love him, who have been called according to his purpose" (Rom. 8:28). I knew that my message to audiences would have to include more than just Jadyn's rescue. From that point forward I would include the hope available for men and women facing unimaginable tragedy. Soon I would discover how desperate the world was to hear about that hope.

It was with great trepidation that I added the message of "what if" in telling Jadyn's story. How could I speak with authority about loss? My granddaughter had been returned to me alive and well. Surely there would be people in the audience who had lost a child or faced some other unspeakable heartache. Would they be hurt or offended when I, who had been so blessed, spoke of hope? Yet I was compelled to share what I knew to be true.

I made the first presentation of living fully alive including the what-if challenge at the annual Gaither Family Fest in Gatlinburg, Tennessee. The response was overwhelming. Afterward I stood in the hallway for over an hour greeting people who'd listened to my talk and wanted to thank me for my words, ask a question, or share their personal stories. I would never again hesitate to share my message.

It was there that I met Ron Pierce, a tall, handsome man

who took me aside and told me the incredible story of his son Happy. As a devoted father and grandfather, I'm always moved by stories of children who live fully alive while they're still young. Some of them achieve St. Irenaeus's goal of living "fully and eternally alive" while adults around them are still trying to "find themselves."

Hearing Ron's story was divine confirmation that I must continue to proclaim Christ as our hope for living and our only hope for finding joy in the presence of soul-numbing tragedy.

Ron and his wife, Brenda, lived in Mobile, Alabama, with their two sons and three daughters. After Ron returned from Operation Desert Storm, where he served in the chaplaincy of the National Guard, he was at Camp Shelby, Mississippi, during the spring of 1996 for summer camp. He made a quick trip home to celebrate his birthday with his family, including his sixteen-year-old son, Happy Lee.

Scarcely old enough to drive, Happy was a living example of his name. He inspired all who knew him. He was the team chaplain as well as a valued player on his school football, basketball, and baseball teams. Happy's baseball skills had caught the attention of college scouts; his season batting average was .438. It looked like a scholarship might enable Happy to go to college anywhere he wanted. The day Ron came home for his birthday party, Happy played an all-star double-header with college scouts watching from the stands. Ron said that after the games that day, Happy came home, cleaned up, and went out again, this time with his sister Charity. The two of them were talented line dancers who'd caught the eye of the company asked to do the choreography for the opening of the Junior Miss competition (now called Distinguished Young Women) telecast in Mobile every year. They had invited Happy and Charity to teach the contestants a dance for the opening number on the broadcast, so off they went that night to practice the moves they would teach the girls.

It was late when Happy called his dad to say they were on the way home and he would pick up some fast food for dinner. Ron had to be back at Camp Shelby early the next morning to lead chapel services, so he put on his uniform and dozed on the couch, waiting for the kids to come home with his meal.

A knock at the door woke him up. He remembered later that as he walked across the room that night he thought, *I'm not eating tacos at this time of the night.*

When Ron opened the door, a state trooper stood on the front porch. "Are you Mr. Pierce?" he asked.

"Yes."

"Your son and daughter have been in a terrible car accident. You need to get to the hospital. Neither one of them is expected to make it."

Ron and Brenda rushed to the hospital. Charity was stabilized after eighteen hours of surgery, but the doctors gave them little hope for Happy.

"I stayed there beside him day after day," Ron told me. "Other than his head injury he looked fine. He seemed so calm. I prayed from the depth of my soul. I claimed all of God's promises for him and expected Happy to open his eyes any minute. Our God is an awesome God. I knew everything was going to be all right."

Happy lived for nine days.

"When they told me he was gone," Ron said, "we donated all of his organs because he had told us that's what he wanted. Even at sixteen he had decided that if something happened to him he wanted other people to be able to have their needs answered."

"I preached my own son's funeral," Ron told me, pausing to regain his composure. "One of my son's favorite songs was 'If

You Could See Me Now' by Kim Noblitt, which was actually written originally for a funeral. I wanted to have it performed at Happy's service and called the writer to get his permission. 'No, I'll do better than that,' he said, 'I'll sing it myself.' And Kim Noblitt flew from Nashville at his own expense to sing at Happy's funeral."

Over 2,700 people attended the funeral or visited the funeral home—classmates, teammates, peers who knew Happy from his role as a team chaplain, others he had invited to church or visited at home if he knew they were having problems. Happy had touched that many lives that deeply in only sixteen years. He had lived more fully alive in those few years than many people who live five times as long. Not only was his life full of the joy of accomplishment and honor, by his example he brought the message of Christ's love to thousands. And there were more to come.

Happy's death was a crisis of faith for Ron. "I was ready to quit when he died," Ron admitted. "I didn't deal with it the way most Christians say they deal with things. I got angry with God. I mean, here was a boy who was giving his life to the Lord and doing everything a young man should do. I had claimed all the promises. Why would God allow this to happen?"

Inundated by well-wishers, Ron and his family accepted an offer to get away for a while to the Colorado mountains. "You could hear your heart beat, it was so quiet," Ron recalled. "It helped my children and my wife, but I was still angry."

When Ron came home, he felt he couldn't put his heart into preaching anymore. He and Brenda had long talks about it. "How can I go back in the pulpit and tell people to stand on the promises when they didn't work for me?" he asked her. "Wouldn't I be a hypocrite to stand up there and tell them something that I didn't find true in my own life and in the life of my son?"

For two months, he didn't preach. During that time his church brought in visiting pastors and kept paying his salary. Brenda wouldn't hear of him giving up. "You listen to me," she said. "You are going to preach. Those people have held that pulpit for you and paid you this whole time. You owe it to them to go over there and preach at least one more time."

Ron agreed to preach one final message. He set out to prepare the worst sermon possible so the congregation would say, "He's lost it," and fire him. It would be communion Sunday, so his sermon had to be shorter than he'd originally planned. He tore a page out of a daily devotional guide and read it from the pulpit word for word—no feeling, no passion, just a recitation of empty words.

"Then," he said, "I stepped down behind the communion table. I lifted my hands and said the simplest thing I could think of: 'As you are coming to the table, remember, "For God so loved the world that He gave—"'" Ron began to weep that day, just as he now wept telling me the story. "I couldn't go any further.

"I told my congregation, 'The person who needs to repent is me. I've been so angry at God. I forgot that He had to watch His own Son die and that He could have used all the promises in His Word to save Him but He didn't. The reason is because we would have no hope if He had kept His Son from dying. I need to repent.'" Ron fell to his knees in front of the church and asked God to forgive him for his anger. That day became one of the most remarkable days of worship the church had ever known. It marked the beginning of new spiritual growth, an increase in membership, and Ron's ministry catching on fire.

Soon afterward Ron got an offer to be a law-enforcement chaplain. But how could he change careers right as his church was really taking off? He turned it down. Then that night he heard a voice in his heart saying, *I don't carry you through anything I don't want to use you for.* Ron knew he had to use his experience to bring hope to others. He called back the next day and asked how much of the job would be counseling people who had lost loved ones.

"About 65 percent," the woman on the phone told him. "You will make all death notifications. You will be called to all homicides, suicides, death-by-fire, death-by-drowning. You will minister to the families of attempted suicides. You will work with them and help them get through the crisis until you can get help for them—permanently if they need it."

This was the job that his son's death had prepared him for. He accepted even though he dreaded the thought of being on call twenty-four hours a day. Later, someone who appreciated what he was doing in the community sent Ron and his wife to the Bill Gaither Family Fest.

"Those were the three most wonderful days of my life," Ron said joyfully. "I cried. I clapped. I stomped my feet. I did everything." It was at one of the meetings there that Ron heard my story and shared his own. We have become friends.

Ron's spiritual journey mirrored some of the things I had talked about at Family Fest that night: in spite of disappointment or even terrible loss, God can do powerful things in every life. Ron knew that, too, because of what his son's life—and death—had taught him. Happy had inspired 2,700 people enough to come to his funeral. Now he had inspired Ron to take a difficult job comforting people in their moments of loss. Ron's ministry was a part of the legacy of his son. Every angry, hopeless person in Mobile who had to endure the tragic, often violent, loss of someone close was blessed by Ron and, through him, by the son whose life inspired his ministry.

Today the double-depth file drawer in Chaplain Pierce's desk is stuffed, not with file folders but with cards and letters from people he has ministered to—"families who, because of the death of my son and the ministry he inspired me to do, I've been able to help through their crisis." And it's still not over!

One of the things I love about Ron is his honesty. Happy Lee Pierce died more than fifteen years ago, yet Ron freely admits that the pain is still close to the surface. He wept openly as he talked about losing his son. He misses him to this day. That truth is a reminder to Ron that faith in Christ doesn't make the waves of sorrow disappear. "We still have tears," Ron says of his family. "We also have great times of laughter. Happy was the type of person who was just so wonderful. He touched the lives of everybody who ever knew him. His memory brings us joy."

Suddenly Ron's finger stabs the air. "And here's something important to remember: my son was not punished. He was rewarded with heaven early. I am a better father, a better minister, a better husband because of the loss of my son. I never would have gone into law enforcement, I never would have helped these thousands of people, had Happy not gone to heaven early. It was only when I felt the Lord saying to me, *I don't carry you through anything I don't want to use you for . . . here's an open door . . . you need to walk through this door*, that I took on this work.

"A lady said to me, 'Oh, Happy had such potential. Too bad he didn't live up to his greatest potential.' I said, 'No ma'am, my son absolutely lived up to his greatest potential, the greatest potential of all of my children—to enter the kingdom of God.'"

Ron tells people based on his own experience, "You will not understand anything in that terrible moment. Don't try to sort it out." In their shock, anger, and pain, people have screamed at Ron, hit him, and knocked him down. But he knows all about that anger and knows that absorbing it and forgiving them is part of his ministry.

On one memorable call, Ron went to tell a woman her son had committed suicide. She was sitting on the sidewalk, waiting for the news.

"I walked out there and knelt down in front of her," he said, then started to tell her what happened. "'There is no easy way to say this . . .'"

That was as far as he got before she hit him with a right hook, screaming at the top of her lungs. Ron crawled back to his feet and held up his hand.

"Don't you talk to me!" she yelled. "If you haven't lost a son, you have no right to talk to me!"

Ron replied, "Then what is it you want me to say?"

"You lost a son?"

"Yes, ma'am."

The woman collapsed in tears. Ron held her and let her cry. After a long moment she asked, "Tell me, how am I going to make it?"

"You're going to make it one step at a time," Ron answered, "one step at a time with the power of God."

And so another life was touched and transformed by the power of one sixteen-year life fully lived.

"At the end of the funeral we played the song that he liked to sing, 'I lay all my trophies down,'" Ron remembered. "We didn't have a clue how many people he had touched. You don't have a clue."

Then Ron added his voice to hundreds of others who have responded to the "what if" portion of my message. "Address reality," he said. "Let people who are in the midst of the most horrible tragedy and pain know there is hope.

"Keep challenging people to live fully alive," he said. "Keep telling them of the hope they have in Christ. Honor my son by telling the story of how he lived fully alive. Don't ever stop."

And to Ron I say, dear friend, the legacy of Happy's life still isn't over. Every reader of this book will know of his commitment. The truth that made him live so fully alive and helped him reach his full potential continues to be spread. In his honor, in honor of the One who brought your son joy unspeakable, I will not stop!

Chapter Eighteen

NOW IS THE TIME, AND YOU ARE THE ONE

WHEN I WAS AT MY HEAVIEST, I REMEMBER SITTING DOWN one night in front of the television and eating a smoked salmon. That's right, an entire salmon packed in some kind of oil. This was no ordinary 10W-30. This was pure "cholester-oil." Afterward I sat in the chair, unable to get up. I had this strange, overpowering urge to swim upstream and lay eggs. I continued my gluttony throughout the Thanksgiving and Christmas holidays. Since I didn't have to make any presentations, I waddled around in sweatpants, eating chocolates and nuts and cookies that well-meaning but evil people had sent us as Christmas gifts. The first clue to weight gain is tight-fitting clothes, but sweatpants never get tight. They expand as you do.

In January Diane and I boarded a cruise ship where I was scheduled to do a show each night. It had been a long time since I'd been on stage. I had no idea how much weight I had gained until we unpacked the performance clothes I had not worn for months. I panicked as I lay in my cabin, squirming to get the button and the buttonhole on my trousers somewhere near each other. Finally I took a deep breath and managed to get the pants buttoned. My performance that night was anxious and measured. I knew that if the button let go, it could kill someone in the front row. It was shortly after this that I saw the picture of myself on the beach and realized that if change was going to happen, I had to do something *now.*

It's so easy to agree in principle to the steps that are necessary to live fully alive, yet still nothing happens. Three weeks later we're in the same rut. Years go by without any appreciable change. Rather than moving forward, sometimes our progress is measured in sliding backward. My Baptist friends call it backsliding; my old missionary friend called it "mossy butt." We give up on keeping physically fit and decide to concede the victory to gravity, the root word of which is *grave.* Opportunity after opportunity to live slips through our fingers. We find it easier to watch TV than study or drive the few miles to visit with a neighbor. We think about what needs to be done but never do it.

If you want to live fully alive, *now* is the time to take action, and *you* are the only one who can do it.

TROUBLE WITH FROGS

Procrastination is another one of those vampires that sucks the blood from living fully alive. One of the most amazing examples of procrastination is in the book of Exodus. Moses and Aaron had pleaded with the pharaoh of Egypt to let the people of God go. God had unleashed two horrible plagues on Egypt. First He turned all the water to blood. Then He released a plague of frogs.

Each time, Pharaoh was given an opportunity to stop the plagues and experience the blessing of God. Listen to what Pharaoh did with his opportunity.

There were frogs everywhere. They were in the palace, they were in the bedroom and the kitchen, they were jumping on the people, they were in the food. Finally the plague was so troublesome that Pharaoh summoned Moses and Aaron and begged, "Pray to the Lord to take the frogs away from me and my people, and I will let your people go."

Now this is the part that blows me away. Moses said to Pharaoh, "When do you want me to pray to the Lord to take these frogs away?"

And Pharaoh said, "Tomorrow."

Tomorrow? This man had frogs all over the place, political pressure from every quarter, and domestic pressure beyond imagination. And he decided to spend another night with the frogs?

Pharaoh's "tomorrow" eventually turned into untold suffering for his people. They went through a plague of blood, a plague of frogs, a plague of gnats, a plague of flies, a plague of dying livestock, a plague of horrible boils, a plague of hail, a plague of locusts, a plague of darkness, and finally the worst plague of all: Pharaoh's procrastination eventually led to the death of every firstborn child in Egypt who was not covered by the blood of the Passover.

Exodus 12:29–30 says, "At midnight the LORD struck down all the firstborn in Egypt, from the firstborn of Pharaoh, who sat on the throne, to the firstborn of the prisoner, who was in the dungeon, and the firstborn of all the livestock as well. . . . There was not a house without someone dead." God had brought Pharaoh an opportunity. Now was the time, and he was the one. Pharaoh squandered it.

But wait. His behavior sounds a bit familiar. I've done the same thing. I've passed up God-given opportunity to make changes that could have saved me and the people I love a lot of pain. More than once I have hesitated to take advantage of God's forgiveness and power and have spent another night with the frogs. Sometimes I hear people mock the old message that "God has a wonderful plan for your life." But it's true. The plan is for you to know Him, and His forgiveness, and the power of His resurrection in your life. The plan is for you to live fully alive.

But He doesn't force this plan on you. You're the one who has to make the decision to trust Him and take action. I think one of the reasons we get so glib and cynical about the gospel, even about the challenge to live fully alive, is that we forget the alternative. The alternative to living fully alive is being totally dead.

That is the plan Satan has for your life. And his best strategy for achieving his goal is to get you to wait. Wait until tomorrow. Wait until the time is just right. Wait for someone else to do it. "One more night with the frogs can't hurt," he whispers.

The Bible says, "Resist the devil, and he will flee from you" (James 4:7). That means more than just turning your back on temptation; it means recognizing that now is the time for action, and you are the one to respond.

In his book *Tide Rising* Bruce Theileman used this illustration:

> It is said that Satan once called to him the emissaries of hell and said he wanted to send one of them to earth to aid women and men in the ruination of their souls. He asked which one would want to go. One creature came forward and said, "I will go." Satan said, "If I send you, what will you tell the children of men?" He said, "I will tell the children of men that there is no heaven." Satan said, "They will not believe you, for there is a bit of heaven in every human heart. In the end

everyone knows that right and good must have the victory. You may not go."

Then another came forward, darker and fouler than the first. Satan said, "If I send you, what will you tell the children of men?" He said, "I will tell them there is no hell." Satan looked at him and said, "Oh, no; they will not believe you, for in every human heart there's a thing called conscience, an inner voice which testifies to the truth that not only will good be triumphant, but that evil will be defeated. You may not go."

Then one last creature came forward, this one from the darkest place of all. Satan said to him, "And if I send you, what will you say to women and men to aid them in the destruction of their souls?"

He said, "I will tell them there is no hurry."

Satan said, "Go!"[1]

Tomorrow never comes. The only tomorrow you have is the one you build by acting today. And those windows of opportunity are often small, like portholes that rust shut when not used. Not knowing what to do is rarely the problem. We know what to do, but we're reluctant to do it. What has God inspired you to do now that you may never have a chance to do again? What is God asking you to do? Nothing will ever happen until you take action. *Now* is the time, and *you* are the one.

Several years ago Diane and I were driving from Boone, North Carolina, back to Tennessee with our daughter Taryn and her husband. Taryn has a heart of gold and never hesitates— okay, rarely hesitates—to reach out to someone in need. On that hot and humid day we stopped to fill up with gas. Parked in one of the pump lanes was an old station wagon with the hood up. A frazzled young mother in a summer dress watched helplessly as transmission fluid dripped from underneath. Restless children holding dripping ice cream cones hung from every window. Ice cream covered their faces, ran down the side of the car, and adorned the upholstery. As Taryn pumped gas into her van, she watched the woman stand back from the engine and brush a wisp of damp hair from her forehead, transferring the grease from her hand onto her face.

I walked over and struck up a conversation. I learned that the woman's husband had left her, and she and her children were moving in with another family. They were almost home when the leaky transmission could no longer be ignored. Out of money and running short on patience, the woman tried to calm her squalling, sticky children as she told her story. I was unaware that Taryn was listening to the entire conversation. She finished pumping gas and called everybody back to the van. As we pulled out of the gas station, a loud metallic crack startled us. I slammed on the brakes and looked back only to realize that Taryn had left the gas nozzle in the tank. As we pulled away, it had snapped back against our van like a monster rubber band.

I jumped out to see what damage had been done. Taryn darted from the car and made a beeline to the stranded woman. We waited as they talked and watched as Taryn started back toward us. The lady shouted something, and Taryn paused to respond. I was feeling lucky that we hadn't caused a fire or hazardous fuel spill. Meanwhile Taryn looked like she'd just won the lottery.

We had to press her to get the story. She told us that as she pumped gas and listened to the woman's story, she was overwhelmed with a conviction to help this woman financially. One hundred dollars was the exact figure she felt God wanted her to give. Opportunity knocked. Then she thought of how foolish she would feel if the woman rejected her gift. How condescending the offer might appear. She decided to pass. The conviction and her inner debate whether to respond or not distracted her so much she forgot to take the nozzle from the tank and return it to the pump.

Taryn said she almost turned inside out when the gas hose snapped. God had given her another chance to act. She flew from the van before it came to a stop. We watched as she gave the woman a hundred-dollar bill and told her it was a gift from God. It would be enough to fill the leaky transmission, buy more sugar for the kids, and maybe have some left over just to remind her that someone cared. We were all in awe of God's presence in that moment. But there was one more question. As Taryn walked back to the car, what had the woman said to her? Taryn paused, her eyes rimmed with tears, "She asked me if I was an angel." I think the answer was yes. God had given Taryn that moment to be an angel in this woman's life, then gave her a rare second chance to experience the blessing of responding.

DON'T BE FOOLED

Now is the time, and *you* are the one. Don't let anyone tell you different. Here are some old sayings that must be ousted as the lies they are.

"There's always tomorrow."

Not true. We don't have any guarantee about tomorrow. We don't even know what the rest of today has in store. We only have this moment.

"Time is on our side."

I have a drawer full of medicine and pictures from my twenty-year class reunion that prove time is not on my side. I also have a kink in my hip that constantly whispers, "Time is not on your side; I am on your side." The Bible confirms that this is a myth. Ecclesiastes 12:1 says, "Remember your Creator in the days of your youth, before the days of trouble come and the years approach when you will say, 'I find no pleasure in them.'" Time is not on your side. Capture the moment.

"Good things come to those who wait."

In reality, good things come to those who wait on the Lord. Once He speaks, the waiting is over. Your dreams or your nightmares will be a result of what you do with this moment, and the next, and the next. *Now* is the time for action, and *you* are the one to take the first step.

After three months of training vigorously for the triathlon, I was making my way once again up the long hill from the Natchez Trace to my home. I had already ridden almost twenty miles and was pleased to feel my body respond to the challenge of making it to the top of the same hill that, only months before, had been the site of complete exhaustion. As I rounded the final curve and could see the summit, I heard a noise behind me. It reminded me of those old artificial lung machines as they expelled air with a prolonged hiss and then quickly sucked in air with a gasping sound.

Hissss. *Guh*. Hissss. *Guh*.

I glanced behind me and saw what looked like a fossil of a man peddling up the hill. And the old guy was gaining on me! The sound I heard was his labored breathing. My competitive spirit kicked in. This guy was older than I was—there was no way I could let him beat me to the top of the hill. I stood up and began to crank on the pedals as hard as I could.

Hissss. *Guh*. Hissss. *Guh*.

The sound got louder. Out of the corner of my eye I watched in horror as the man pulled out to pass me. By then I was making some pretty desperate sucking sounds of my own. He was beside me now. I hoped he couldn't hear the sound of my ego deflating as he purposely slowed his pace to match mine. I was still pretty certain that he was older than I was, but there was nothing old about the light in his eyes.

"Don't stop doing this," he said.

I said nothing . . . I was too busy sucking air to speak.

"I do this to live," he continued. "I don't do it to stay alive. I do it to live!"

I suppose I should have been inspired by his words, but all I could think was, *How can this man talk and ride at this pace at the same time?* Then with the enthusiasm of someone who has just won an Oscar, he announced, "This is the anniversary of my stroke. I had lost my ability to speak, but now I've got it back. I still haven't regained full use of my left arm or leg, but I'm alive!" A huge smile glowed from beneath his grey beard. "Don't ever stop doing this," he said. Then he bent over into that bicycle racing position and left me like I was standing still.

As he reached the top of the hill, he looked over his shoulder and shouted, "*Live!*" Then he disappeared.

I hear his voice often as I face some challenge or when I'm tempted to coast instead of peddle. *Live!* That word inspired this book. The glory of God is man fully alive: Striving in the midst of all odds. Never satisfied with the status quo. Seeking excellence in every area of life. Because Jesus can raise the dead and because He Himself was raised from the dead, then no matter what my situation, I can know the power of His resurrection to live my life fully alive.

So as you consider the first steps you will take toward a new kind of life, I'm acutely aware that there will be times of struggle, valleys of doubt and despair. There will be times when tragedy threatens to derail you. There will be times when you'll be tempted to give up or wait until tomorrow. In the midst of those times, if you listen carefully, you will hear a sound.

Hissss. *Guh.* Hissss. *Guh.*

That sound will be me, coming up behind you with a simple word of encouragement: *Now* is the time, and *you* are the one.

Live!

For God's sake, live!

IT'S ALL ABOUT
THE MATH

YOU WOULD THINK THAT AFTER YEARS OF WORKING TO
stay healthy, I would have developed a natural "feel" for how
much food to eat and how much exercise to do. You would think
wrong. The only natural inclination I have is to sit on my butt
and eat enormous amounts of food that I don't need and isn't
good for me. I have no intention of giving you a new diet. But
if you want to step into a new world where you feel fully alive, I
can tell you it comes down to math. Eat fewer calories than you
burn, and you lose weight. Eat more calories than you burn, and
you gain weight. Eat the same number of calories you burn, and
you will stay basically the same.

Eat healthier food and avoid processed foods, and you can
eat more. I can have a great salad with five ounces of chicken
and some wonderful fruit and vegetables thrown in. Top it off
with a low-calorie dressing or salsa (dressing on the side please),
and I have consumed less than 400 calories, and I feel full. Or I

can snarf down two of my favorite candy bars totaling over 500 calories and still be hungry for more. Lean closer—here's my secret. I know that if I don't do anything but sit at a computer and write this book, my body burns between 1,800 and 2,000 calories a day. I also know that depending on what exercise I do, if I work at keeping my heart rate up for about an hour, I will burn between 500 and 1,000 calories more. If I add the amount of calories I burn doing exercise to the amount I burn by sitting in a chair, I come up with the number of calories I can eat that day without gaining weight.

Here's an example.

If I run for an hour, I burn 800 calories. If I sit at the computer all day, I burn 1,800. Add the two together, and I know that I can eat 2,600 calories that day and stay even. I always eat a little less just to be safe. If I want to lose about a pound a week, I eat 500 fewer calories a day than I burn. So on this day I could eat 2,100 calories and still be on track to lose about a pound a week. Women have a different metabolism than men. Older people burn fewer calories than younger ones. So how do you know what you burn, and how do you find out how many calories are in the foods you eat? Why won't you find it in this book?

First, this is not primarily a weight-loss book. There are hundreds of helpful books and programs that will enable you to calculate the amount of calories your body burns in a normal day. You are only one click away from many other Internet resources that calculate calories for you. The key is this: keep it simple. If you can't make it simple, you will stop doing it. In this book I talk about the importance of keeping a journal. If you want to be fully alive physically, it's going to take a little research and experimentation to get it right. My friend Phil knows that with his lifestyle he can lose weight by eating 1,200 calories a day. My lifestyle allows about 1,500 a day on average.

Second, if you are not willing to do a little research and discipline yourself to find out how your body works, I can almost guarantee you won't be willing to do the other work that leads to living fully alive. I know. I'm just like you. Here are a few hints that you might find helpful as well:

- Avoid food that comes in a box.
- If you don't know what's on your plate, don't eat it. You may know exactly how many calories are in that slab of salmon, but you may be shocked to find out how many are in the sauce it's swimming in.
- Practice portion control. Just because chicken is good for you doesn't mean you can eat a whole chicken. Know portion sizes, and eat small portions.
- Eat slowly and chew your food. It tastes better that way. It's amazing how much more accurately you can detect when you are full when you eat slowly.
- If you drink alcohol, take it easy. Alcohol is basically empty calories. I know you've heard that a glass of wine is good for you. They didn't mean a glass bottle. They meant about four ounces.
- Develop meals you are familiar with and stick with them. I have four or five options for each meal of the day. I don't have to add up the calories for each ingredient. I know the calories in the entire meal. When I eat out, I also tend to order foods that I enjoy and am familiar with. If I don't know what is in a sauce or a side dish, I ask. If I can't calculate its nutritional value, I don't order it.
- Here is a new one: eat lots of green vegetables. Fortunately I love most of them and have discovered ways to cook them that make them every bit as delightful as some of the sexier but less healthy foods available.

- Write it before you bite it. One of the most helpful disciplines I learned was to plan the meals I was going to eat and record the calories ahead of time.
- Stop eating after dinner.
- Don't ever snack while watching television.
- Once a week, give yourself a break. Once you experience the benefits of healthy eating, you will find little pleasure in gluttony. But you will find great pleasure in that single piece of chocolate.
- When you fall off the wagon, get right back on. I can't tell you how many times I have slipped up. But I love living fully alive more than I love food. I've got my eyes on the prize, so I will not give up.
- Finally, hide the chocolate!

For over a year I wore a device on my arm that recorded every calorie I burned. I kept a record of that data and now have the ability to tell you within ten calories how much I burn with any exercise I do. Then, because I have a tendency to get lazy and to forget the little things I put in my mouth, I use an application on my phone that allows me to enter my weight goals, my exercise, and the food that I eat. The app is called "My Fitness Pal." It's free, and it calculates the calories in my food and the calories burned in exercise.

There are other resources that keep detailed track of all the nutritional values of the food you eat. If you are anything like me, don't try to wing it.

When someone told me that nuts were good for you, I did a little celebration dance. I love nuts. There were bowls of almonds and pistachios and walnuts scattered around the house. One day I decided to track the exact number of calories in the nuts I was eating. I was snacking on over 750 calories of nuts every day.

Nuts! It's back to that mistaken principle that if a little is good, then a lot is better. I still eat nuts, but I write 'em before I bite 'em.

My wife, Diane, is the one who taught me to "write it before I bite it," though she uses a different method of calculation. She has benefited greatly from a program called Weight Watchers. It doesn't matter what method or Internet tool you use, as long as you keep track. Vigilance and consistency make the difference.

Appendix 2

THERE'S AN APP FOR THAT

HERE ARE A FEW OF THE RESOURCES THAT HAVE HELPED ME regain my physical health. This is not an exhaustive list. My desire is to get you started. After you're on your way, do your own research. New books and apps are coming out almost daily. If it works for you, use it. Also remember that strict diets don't work. Keep it simple; keep it flexible. Just like we rest one day a week, let up on your eating habits one day a week. You'll quickly find that you prefer healthy eating to gorging yourself on your day off.

BOOKS

Body for Life: 12 Weeks to Mental and Physical Strength
by Bill Phillips (William Morrow, 1999)

This book on exercise and nutrition can help you establish lifestyle patterns you can follow for a lifetime. A yearly bodybuilding competition makes following the program interesting. I have no desire to look like a muscle man, but this book helped me design a weight-lifting program that worked. It also features excellent common-sense dietary information. I still reread portions of this book.

The Fat Burning Diet: Accessing Unlimited Energy for a Lifetime by Jay Robb (Loving Health Publications, 1999)

Jay Robb personally helped set me on a road back to health by providing practical nutritional advice. I will always be grateful for his counsel and support. As a person who travels, I find protein supplements to be very helpful. Jay's are some of purest available, and his dietary philosophy can be followed for a lifetime. Many meals in my regular diet were designed based on Jay's coaching.

Younger Next Year: Live Strong, Fit, and Sexy–Until You're 80 and Beyond by Chris Crowley and Henry S. Lodge (Workman Publishing, 2007)

This book inspired me to get out of the starting blocks and start taking care of my body. The title is perfect. After three years I feel and act younger than when I read the book. If you follow the exercise plan recommended here, you, too, will be younger next year. My thanks go to Lodge and Crowley for motivating me to regain my physical health.

From Vanity to Health by Keelan Hastings

This is a short read with a powerful punch. Written by my personal trainer, this book gives an overall view of the value of resistance training in maintaining health. The author has helped many people get back on track physically.

SMARTPHONE APPLICATIONS AND INTERNET PROGRAMS

My Fitness Pal

This app is free, easy to use, and accurate. What more could you ask for? It keeps track of calories eaten and calories burned. "My Fitness Pal" allows you to set goals and then track your progress toward those goals. My favorite feature is the ability to scan the bar code on any packaged food and get a readout of calories per serving that you can instantly record for the day. You also can create your own recipes for meals you eat often. Name the meal, enter the ingredients, and from then on it's one click to enter the whole meal.

Fitday.com

If you are really into tracking all the details of nutrition, this is an excellent program.

Livestrong.com

Easy to find calories for just about anything you eat. Unless it's cat food!

BodyBugg: myapexfitness.com

This program is a bit expensive and takes some time to learn, but it will help you develop a very accurate assessment of your metabolism and how many calories you burn each day as well as provide an easy-to-read record of your complete nutritional intake. Telephone coaching is offered early in the program and is invaluable for learning how to use the system. It does require that you wear an armband daily. I found this not to be a problem, except on days I forgot to put it on.

The information then can be entered manually with little loss in accuracy. It also works on any phone that can access the Internet.

WEIGHT-LOSS PROGRAM

Weight Watchers

Of all the weight-loss programs out there, the most realistic and most supportive I have tried is Weight Watchers. The only reason I don't attend now is because my travel schedule makes it impossible. These folks understand the difference between a lifestyle change and a fad diet. Diets don't work. Realistic lifestyle changes that can be maintained for a lifetime are the key to continued health. My wife, Diane, has greatly benefited from the supportive friends and advice she gets at Weight Watchers.

BOTTOM LINE

First and most important: start moving today. Don't limit your movement to physical exercise. Move toward being more alive socially, mentally, and spiritually. Seek excellence in every area of your life.

NOTES

CHAPTER 2: A WILD RIDE IN A SHALLOW BATHTUB

1. Dave Barry, *Dave Barry Is Not Taking This Sitting Down* (New York: Ballantine Books, 2001), 153.
2. Quoted in Denis Minn, *Irenaeus: An Introduction* (United Kingdom: T&T Clark Int'l, 2010), 75.
3. Trace Adkins, vocal performance of "Dangerous Man," by Brad Crisler and Craig Wiseman, on *Dangerous Man*, released August 15, 2006, Capitol Nashville, compact disc.
4. Switchfoot, vocal performance of "Awakening," by Jon Foreman, on *Oh! Gravity*, released on March 26, 2007, Columbia/SONY BMG, compact disc.
5. *The Princess Bride*, directed by Rob Reiner (1987; Beverly Hills, CA: MGM, 2000), DVD.

CHAPTER 3: THE POWER CURVE

1. G. K. Chesterton, "When Doctors Agree," *Paradoxes of Mr Pond* (Kelly Bray, Cornwall, UK: House of Stratus, 2008), 41.

CHAPTER 5: BODY COUNTS

1. Cynthia L. Ogden, PhD, et al., "Prevalence of Obesity in the United States, 2009–2010," National Center for Health Statistics Data Brief, no. 82, January 2012, CDC, http://www.cdc.gov /nchs/data/databriefs/db82.htm.
2. "Obesity Related Statistics in America," Get America Fit Foundation, http://www.getamericafit.org/statistics-obesity -in-america.html.
3. Keelan Hastings, *From Vanity to Health* (self-published brochure, 2009), 8.
4. Chris Crowley and Henry S. Lodge, M.D., *Younger Next Year* (New York: Workman Publishing Company, 2007).
5. Dan Buettner, "How to Live to Be 100," TED, http://www.ted .com/talks/danbuettnerhowtolivetobe100.html.
6. Crowley and Lodge, *Younger Next Year*, 30.
7. Ibid.

CHAPTER 6: NO EXCUSES

1. Mike Flynt, *The Senior: My Amazing Year as a 59-Year-Old College Football Linebacker* (Nashville: Thomas Nelson, Inc., 2008).
2. Caroline Davies, "World's oldest marathon runner completes Toronto race at age 100," *The Guardian*, October 17, 2011, http:// www.guardian.co.uk/uk/2011/oct/17/worlds-oldest-marathon -runner-100.
3. Christopher Reeve, *Nothing Is Impossible*: *Reflections on a New Life* (New York: The Random House Publishing Group, 2002), 88, 190.
4. Quoted in Bob Lodie, "It's All About Beliefs," *The Small Business Brief,* newsletter, http://www.smallbusinessbrief.com/articles /inspiration/003753.html#top.

CHAPTER 8: FROM POLE TO POLE

1. Chris Crowley and Henry S. Lodge, M.D., *Younger Next Year* (New York: Workman Publishing Company, 2007), 135.
2. Anne Lamott, *Bird by Bird* (New York: Anchor Books, 1995), 19.

3. Bill Phillips, *Body for Life: 12 Weeks to Mental and Physical Strength* (New York: Harper Collins, 1999).

CHAPTER 9: ONE IS A LONELY NUMBER

1. Bill Gothard, *Institute in Basic Life Principles* (Oak Brook, IL: IBLP, 1989), 167.

CHAPTER 10: FINDING YOUR SWEET SPOT

1. Rick Warren, *The Purpose Driven Life* (Grand Rapids: Inspirio, 2003), 11.
2. Ted Turner, *20/20* interview with Barbara Walters, c. 1995.
3. George Clooney, *Piers Morgan Tonight*, interview with Piers Morgan on Sudan, the US Media, and Politics, CNN, January 22, 2011, http://www.youtube.com/watch?v=UceKpupul_g.

CHAPTER 11: LIGHTEN UP!

1. Anne Lamott, *Bird by Bird* (New York: Anchor Books, 1995), xviii.
2. Dynamic Communicators Workshops, http://www.scorreconference.com.

CHAPTER 13: PRESS ON

1. Adapted from Ken Davis, *How to Speak to Youth . . . and Keep Them Awake at the Same Time* (Grand Rapids: Zondervan, 1996), 104–106.

CHAPTER 15: WHAT'S LOVE GOT TO DO WITH IT?

1. Jackie DeShannon, vocal performance of "What the World Needs Now Is Love," by Hal David and Burt Bacharach, released April 15, 1965, Imperial Records, LP.

CHAPTER 18: NOW IS THE TIME, AND YOU ARE THE ONE

1. Bruce Theileman, *Tide Rising*, excerpt no. 30, http://www.preachingtoday.com.

ABOUT THE AUTHOR

KEN DAVIS, BEST-SELLING AUTHOR AND FREQUENT RADIO and television guest, is a sought-after speaker. His mixture of side-splitting humor and inspiration delights and enriches audiences of all ages.

Ken has been keynote speaker for hundreds of church and major corporate events, and he has made thousands of personal appearances around the world. As president of Dynamic Communications International, he teaches speaking skills to ministry professionals and corporate executives. Ken's daily radio show *Lighten Up!* is heard on more than 1,500 stations in the United States and around the world.

Ken is a graduate of Oak Hills Christian College. He and his wife, Diane, live in Tennessee and have two daughters and six grandchildren. The entire family is involved in Ken's ministry, bringing much laughter and liberating truth to people all across the globe.

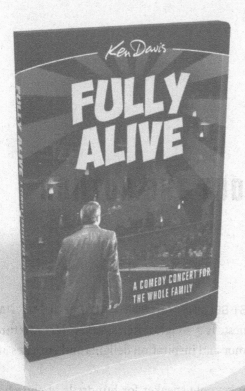

NOTES

1. Bill Buford, *Among the Thugs: 12 Weeks in Moscow with a Strange Loyalty* (New York: Vintage/Collins, 1990).

CHAPTER 9: ONE IS A LONELY NUMBER

1. Bill Gothard, seminar in basic life principles (Oak Brook, Ill: IBLP, 1983), 10.

CHAPTER 10: FINDING YOUR SWEET SPOT

1. Kurk Warner, *The Inquest Direct by Christian's guide* (Inspire, 2001), 11.
2. "Interview," CNN interview with Barbara Walters, c. 1995.
3. George Clooney, "Interview, George's interview with Marc Cooper on Sudan, the US, Darfur and Rwanda," CNN, January 22, 2007, http://www.worldis.com/arc.html/transcript.

CHAPTER 11: LIGHTEN UP

1. Anne Lamott, *Bird by Bird* (New York: Anchor Books, 1995), xvii.
2. Dynamite Communications Workshops, http://www.hotpasskiterence.com

CHAPTER 12: PRESS ON

1. Adapted from Ken Davis, *How to Speak to Youth . . . and Keep Them Awake at the Same Time* (Grand Rapids, Mich.: Zondervan, 1996), 239–240.

CHAPTER 16: WHAT'S LOVE GOT TO DO WITH IT?

1. Jackie Robinson, vocal performance of "What the World Needs Now Is Love," Paul Lahti Dorsey and Paul Backman, released April 15, 1967, Imperial records 67.

CHAPTER 18: NOW IS THE TIME, AND YOU ARE THE ONE

1. About *Thailand*, wiki Rising, excerpt on 50, http://www.preachingtoday.com.